A KNITTER'S GUIDE TO
Shawl Design

A KNITTER'S GUIDE TO
Shawl Design

Emma Vining

THE CROWOOD PRESS

First published in 2021 by
The Crowood Press Ltd
Ramsbury, Marlborough
Wiltshire SN8 2HR

enquiries@crowood.com

www.crowood.com

British Library Cataloguing-in-Publication Data
A catalogue record for this book is available from the British Library.

ISBN 978 1 78500 963 1

Cover design: Maggie Mellett

Typeset by Jean Cussons Typesetting, Diss, Norfolk
Printed and bound in India by Parksons Graphics

CONTENTS

ABBREVIATIONS AND CHART SYMBOLS

Abbreviations

dec'd: decreased

inc'd: increased

k: knit

k2tog: knit the next two stitches together (1st dec'd)

k2tog-tbl: knit the next two stitches together through the backs of their loops (1st dec'd)

k3tog: knit the next three stitches together (2sts dec'd)

m1 and m1l: make one and make one left – make 1 stitch by bringing the tip of the left-hand needle from front to back under the strand of yarn running between the stitches sitting closest to the tips of the left- and right-hand needles and then knitting through the back of this loop (1st inc'd)

m1r: make one right – make 1 stitch by bringing the tip of the left-hand needle from back to front under the strand of yarn running between the stitches sitting closest to the tips of the left- and right-hand needles and then knitting this loop (1st inc'd)

mrk: stitch marker

p: purl

p2tog: purl the next two stitches together (1st dec'd)

p2tog-tbl: purl the next two stitches together through the backs of their loops (1st dec'd)

p3tog: purl the next three stitches together (2sts dec'd)

patt: pattern, work in pattern

pm: place marker

psso: pass slipped stitch over, often worked as a part of a decrease such as 'sl1, k2tog, psso' or 'sl1, p2tog, psso'

rep: repeat

RS: right side or right-side

sk2po: slip 1st, k2tog, pass slipped st over – slip the next stitch from the left-hand needle to the right-hand needle knitwise, knit the next two stitches together (k2tog), and pass the slipped stitch over the first stitch on the right-hand needle (2sts dec'd)

sl1: slip one stitch (purlwise) – slip the next stitch from the left-hand needle to the right-hand needle purlwise, unless working the slipped stitch as part of a 'sl1, k2tog, psso' decrease, in which case slip this stitch knitwise

sl1 wyif: slip one stitch (purlwise) with yarn in front (wyif) – slip the next stitch from the left-hand needle to the right-hand needle purlwise while the yarn is held at the front of the work

sl2: slip two stitches (knitwise) – slip the next 2sts from the left-hand needle to the right-hand needle, one at a time, knitwise

SR(s): short row(s) or short-row

ssk: slip, slip, knit – slip the next 2sts from the left-hand needle to the right-hand needle, one at a time, knitwise; insert the left-hand needle into the fronts of these 2sts at the same time; knit these 2sts together through the backs of their loops (k2tog-tbl) (1st dec'd)

st(s): stitch(es)

w&t: wrap and turn, used with short-row (SR) shaping; a stitch is wrapped to avoid a gap remaining in the knitting where each short row is worked. This wrapping action is known as wrap and turn. To wrap a stitch, knit to the stitch to be wrapped; slip the next stitch purlwise; take the yarn to the back of the work; slip the slipped stitch back to the left-hand needle purlwise without working it; take the yarn to the front of the work; and turn the work. When the wrapped stitch is reached on the subsequent row, work the wrap loop and the wrapped stitch together, to close the gap between the wrapped stitch and the adjacent stitch

WS: wrong side or wrong-side

wyif: with yarn in front

yo: yarn over – take the yarn over the right-hand needle from front to back (1st inc'd)

yo twice: yarn over twice – take the yarn over the right-hand needle twice, and, on the next row, work k1, p1 (or p1, k1, as required for pattern) into the double-yarn-over loop (2sts inc'd)

Symbol	Abbreviation	Description
	k	knit on RS; purl on WS
●	p	purl on RS; knit on WS
	kfb	knit into the front and then the back of the next stitch on the left-hand needle, then allow this knitted-into stitch to slip off of the left-hand needle point (1st inc'd)
/	k2tog	knit the next two stitches together (1st dec'd)
⑪	mb	make bobble by knitting into the next stitch on the left-hand needle as specified in the pattern
V	sl	slip 1st from the left-hand needle to the right-hand needle purlwise, unless working the slipped stitch as part of a 'sl1, k2tog, psso' decrease, in which case slip this stitch knitwise
\	ssk	slip the next two stitches from the left-hand needle to the right-hand needle, one at a time, knitwise; insert the left-hand needle into the front of these two slipped stitches at the same time; knit these two stitches together through the backs of their loops (k2tog-tbl) (1st dec'd)
☐☐		stitch-pattern repeat
○	yo	take the yarn over the right-hand needle from front to back (1st inc'd)
∘∘	yo twice	take the yarn over the right-hand needle twice, and, on the next row, work k1, p1 (or p1, k1, as required for pattern) into the double-yarn-over loop (2sts inc'd)
⊙	yob	take the yarn over the right-hand needle from back to front (backwards) (1st inc'd); where a k2tog, yo sequence is followed by a purl stitch, the yo should be worked by taking the yarn from the back of the work to the front over the right-hand needle, rather than taking the yarn from the front of the work to the back around the right-hand needle as for a working a standard yo. On the following row, work into the back of this yob loop. For further background about yarn overs, *please see* https://ysolda.com/blogs/journal/yarn-overs, on which this explanation is based (with thanks to Ysolda Teague).

Table of chart symbols.

INTRODUCTION

As a hand-knitting designer, I am fascinated by pattern. My favourite patterns are inspired by the world around me, from nature to the built environment. I capture my ideas through sketches and photographs and use these to help me design knitting stitch patterns. Shawl design is the perfect framework in which to place my designs and to explore stitch patterning through the creation of a beautiful, wearable accessory. There are several complete knitting patterns in this book, with full explanations of how the designs were developed through my design process. However, there is so much joy to be found in creating and customizing designs to suit your own preferences. I encourage you to experiment and explore. In this book, my aim is to inspire you to look for your own design source material and to help you to translate your designs into personalized shawls that can be worn, gifted and treasured.

Each chapter throughout this book contains my photographs and sketches of inspirational sources. Examples include archive research, architecture, infrastructure and decorative ironwork. These sources are used to develop ideas for shawl shapes and stitch patterns. Alongside the inspiration, practical advice includes instructions detailing how to knit individual shawl shapes, building up to working with complex combinations of multiple shapes and stitch patterns. With the emphasis on design development, each section contains examples of how different factors affect shawl design. For example, choosing a different yarn fibre can transform a design.

In Part 1 of this book, shawl design is put in a historical context, with illustrations from the Knitting and Crochet Guild (KCG) Collection. By taking a close look at shawls knitted in a variety of what can be considered traditional styles, we can see that knitters have always made their own additions and alterations to established design conventions. Building on these fascinating examples, the next section explores a variety of techniques and tools required for knitting shawls, before going on to consider the effect of using different yarn weights and fibres, and to look at options for edgings and borders.

A fundamental building block of shawl design is the overall shape of the shawl. Part 2 uses inspirational photographs and sketches as a way to approach designing shawl shapes. These shapes are illustrated by knitted swatches, with full instructions provided to recreate the swatches. The emphasis of this section is on the design decisions taken into account when planning a shawl project. Beginning with rectangles and squares, this part goes on to explore triangles, circles, semicircles and crescents.

The final part of this book contains five detailed case studies. Each case study includes the initial inspiration, a detailed description of the shawl's design development and finally the full written knitting pattern. These patterns, and the accompanying images and sketches, along with any of the sections in this book, can be enjoyed as interesting knitting projects. I encourage you to use them as starting points for your own original designs, and I look forward to seeing the results!

What is a Shawl?

The first association with the word 'shawl' is often 'christening', but have you ever come across a 'tippet', a 'wrapper' or a 'cloud'? These terms date from Victorian times, and the accompanying incomplete list shows

Engraving from La Gazette Rose, 15 Octobre 1865, No. 680: Robes et Cachmires, *Louis Berlier, after Héloïse Leloir-Colin, 1865, Rijksmuseum Collection (http://hdl.handle.net/10934/RM0001.COLLECT.490597).*

Shawl with ornamental boteh design, made in Kashmir, France or Great Britain, anonymous, c.1820, Rijksmuseum Collection (http://hdl.handle.net/10934/RM0001.COLLECT.28464).

how much variety there can be in design. When considering the origin of the word 'shawl' in her book *Knitted Shawls and Wraps* (1984), Tessa Lorant explains:

> The word shawl is derived from the Persian 'shal', and was adapted from this into Urdu and other Indian languages. From there it found its way into the European languages in similar forms. However, the term shawl was not in general use in Europe until the end of the seventeenth century, and it did not refer to an article of European dress until almost a century later.

From these early definitions, shawls have developed into extremely popular fashion accessories and even as symbols of status or wealth. Enormous and extremely costly nineteenth-century shawls produced in Paisley, Norwich and Edinburgh were designed to be displayed over the vast, wide skirts fashionable at that time, such as that shown in the accompanying illustration.

More recently, Burberry-monogrammed blanket-size ponchos and iconic Hermès silk scarves are instantly recognizable high-fashion accessories.

A shawl can also be categorized by the material from which it has been made, the construction method used, whether the pattern was woven or printed, and the shape and size of the whole shawl. The accompanying example of the paisley-pattern shawl shows how a single design motif has defined the name of this particular shawl. Although the shawl material could be silk, wool or cotton, it is the presence of this pattern motif that results in the name. Some shawl definitions have been established by long-standing traditional construction methods. However, these methods can overlap. For example, a traditional rectangular shawl can be knitted by using several different methods. It may also include specific stitch patterns typical of a distinct region that are designed specifically to fit within that particular rectangle construction.

When considering why one would ever bother with a

knitted wrap, as opposed to one of an alternative material or fibre, Tessa Lorant tells us:

> Well of course it doesn't have to be knitted; but for keen knitters making some sort of wrap is a delight; even the beginner can learn to make a 'patterned' rectangular wrap without the need to shape or worry about the tension. And an advanced knitter can show intricate pattern knitting off to perfection. Not only that, wraps can be made in thick yarn or in thin, and in knobbly, brushed or other fancy yarn as well as in the ordinary knitting fingerings. They can also be made in different fibres, in many colours, in toning colours, or in a single colour only. The wrap can be embellished with lace edgings, with frills or with flounces, or it can simply be fringed to finish it off.

Knitting a shawl can therefore be considered as a way of experimenting. This can be with a new yarn, an interesting technique or a beautiful stitch pattern. There are a very large number of beautiful and interesting shawl patterns already designed and ready to knit. However, this book is all about creating shawl designs that are truly personal to the knitter or the intended recipient. Bringing new inspiration into shawl design may call for a new set of names and descriptions that reflect the very personal inspiration of the designer and wearer. Although choosing to design your own shawl can at first seem daunting, creating a new and original design is extremely rewarding and enjoyable.

Design Inspiration

Thinking about the particular inspiration and starting points of a shawl in detail can give structure to a project and really help to communicate the design to other knitters. These ideas can be used to spark other ideas for new stitch patterns, shawl shapes or colour schemes. Most importantly, it

List of shawl names

blanket	pelerine
cape	poncho
christening	rebozo
cloud	ruana
comforter	ruffle
crossover	scarf
Estonian	shawl
Faroese	Shetland
fichu	stole
hap	tippet
muffler	veil
neckerchief	wedding
neck handkerchief	wrap
nightingale	wrapper
pashmina	

can help with decision-making during the designing of the whole shawl. The chosen inspiration can feed into some parts only or the whole of the design, affecting the shape, edgings and pattern placements. It is the

Las Setas, Seville, Spain.

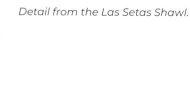

Detail from the Las Setas Shawl.

combination of all of these inspirations together that results in original shawl designs.

Look out for these inspirational elements wherever you go. Carry a notebook, and make sketches and take photos of anything that catches your eye. Tiles, paving stones, railings, flowers, clouds and buildings are just a few examples that can be found in the world around us. Tiny details can be scaled up through design development to become bold patterns. Complex tree branches can be simplified into smooth cable curves. Consider colour, shape and perhaps location. The key point is to feel inspired and think about what has inspired you. For example, the structure, shape and colour of Las Setas in Seville, Spain, inspired the shawl design of the same name. The description and explanation of designing this shawl can be found in Part 3 of this book, along with the full knitting pattern.

Taking inspiration from the world around us can also generate new and exciting ideas. Researching a

Las Setas Shawl.

building or a plant in great detail can reveal interesting facts that can be reflected in the design. By choosing subjects that have an interesting background, a design can become a very personal expression for the knitter. For example, knowing that a plant produces berries in autumn can lead to a series of stitch patterns that include leaf motifs, flower inspiration and berry bobbles. These individual stitch patterns will all relate to each other and are unified through the research undertaken on a single subject.

Another excellent starting point is an exploration of a particular knitting technique such as cable knitting or a style relating to a tradition or geographical region. Research at a museum or heritage collection can provide an excellent framework in which to explore shawl styles, shapes and patterns. Using historical research to inspire a shawl design has the added bene-fit of highlighting techniques that have been in use for a considerable period of time. These techniques can be the building blocks of new designs. The KCG Collection has many beautiful shawls, and a selection of these are considered in detail in this book.

The design can be further developed by using a different yarn weight or fibre, or an additional colour. A stitch pattern can appear completely different when worked in a different yarn or fibre. Small changes can have drastic effects on scale, colour balance and pattern. The effect of different yarn weights and fibres are highlighted throughout this book. Knitted swatches demonstrate the differences that can be achieved, especially in the design-development stages.

Having set the scene for shawl design, the next step is to place shawls in a wider context: Chapter 1 explores shawls through tradition, innovation and inspiration.

Part 1
SHAWL DESIGN IN CONTEXT

CHAPTER 1

TRADITION, INNOVATION AND INSPIRATION

There is a very large number of well-recognized and much-loved traditions in shawl design. Each tradition has its own signature style and construction conventions, in many cases defined by the shape of the shawl and the placement of pattern. However, these distinctive patterns have been amended and adapted over time, to suit the different requirements of different designers, knitters and wearers. Examining the skills and knowledge of knitters over time and in different geographical areas helps us to understand the techniques that were used to create their shawls. Additionally, we can attempt to infer what actually inspired the original shawls and stitch patterns. In many cases, the answer and impetus are a combination of outstanding technical skill, economic necessity and a keen eye for pattern. Tradition, innovation and inspiration are therefore strongly linked and exert equal influence over historical and contemporary shawl design.

In her excellent 2008 book *Knitted Lace of Estonia*, Nancy Bush likens the knitting of a shawl to handwriting, demonstrating the individuality of style within established tradition:

> Although I originally thought that there was a single right way to knit these shawls, I have learned that there are nearly as many ways as there are knitters. Just like handwriting, each knitter has her own way of knitting certain parts of a shawl, and I found that it is quite acceptable to make a change because it worked better for me.

OPPOSITE: Pattern detail from mirror-imaged rectangular shawl, KCG Collection (1998.071.0010).

Commenting on the recording of the shawl patterns, Nancy Bush also highlights a way of passing on information that is common to many traditions:

> The Estonians had no written instructions for their patterns – the techniques and designs were handed down from one generation to the next. Stitch patterns were preserved on long knitted samplers or as individual sample pieces.

The passing on of information in this way allows small changes and customization to be incorporated into the designs, all within the boundaries of the tradition.

Seventy-five individual stitch patterns for Haapsalu shawls were compiled for the beautiful book *Knitted Shawls of Helga Ruutel* (2013). These designs represent only a small selection of approximately 200 charted designs created by Helga Ruutel over several decades. Instantly recognizable as traditional Haapsalu shawls, Helga placed her own individuality into Haapsalu shawl patterns. Her comments reveal that she was very much aware that she was breaking with tradition:

> I changed the yarn overs and decreases of historical shawl patterns. Many thanks to master knitters who did not utter any bad words to a young troublemaker. My wings were not clipped and so, until now, patterns from here and there have been scattered upon my shawls.

These examples clearly demonstrate the importance of the individual in creating traditional patterns. Over time, traditional shawls have been adapted and altered by generations of knitters. Established patterns therefore contain design elements from all of the previous generations of knitters and designers, each bringing their own inspirations and ideas to the traditional practice.

The first section in this chapter explores tradition and innovation in shawl design through selected items held in museums and collections in the United Kingdom (UK). These resources can be accessed either in person or through digital archives. It is important to recognize and to reference techniques and ideas already in existence. This understanding provides the context for new designs. A case study of items from the KCG Collection helps to show the importance of this type of research.

This chapter concludes by placing shawl design in the wider context of fashion. This shows how accessories have been influenced by fashion trends over the years, from simple shapes of a length of cloth wrapped around the wearer for warmth, to elaborate paisley-pattern shawls used to show the wealth and status of the owner. Innovations in technology now allow customization of machine-knitted accessories. However, this book proposes that the ultimate for a customized design is a hand-knitted shawl with a shape, edgings and stitch patterns inspired by sources with personal importance to the designer and wearer.

Museums, Exhibitions and Collections

Researching shawls in museums and archives can really help to achieve a good understanding of traditional styles. This can be undertaken through the handling of items, through the reading of books, leaflets and patterns, and through the viewing of digital archives. There are many excellent resources available for online research and in-person visits. In this section, several examples are considered to demonstrate the breadth of information available in the UK.

The Knitting Reference Library at the University of Southampton Winchester Campus provides a wealth of information for knitters and researchers. Browsing the shelves reveals most of the major knitting styles from over the last hundred years. The online collection of Victorian knitting books takes the reader further back in time and allows the exploration of knitting, crochet and netting during the Victorian era. All of this taken together provides a helpful overview and starting point before exploring new shawl shapes and designs. For example, writing in the second volume of the *Lady's Assistant in Knitting, Netting, and Crochet Work*, Mrs Jane Gaugain provides a pattern for a fichu. As well as a detailed set of written instructions for this small shawl, Mrs Gaugain provides her readers with a schematic diagram. The diagram shows the outline of a

triangular shawl with the addition of a curved notch for the neck. Blocking instructions highlight this feature and show that, although the basic shape of the fichu is a triangle, Mrs Gaugain encourages knitters to adapt the shape for a custom fit.

Entire museum exhibitions have been devoted to particular symbolic shawl styles. The Fashion and Textile Museum (FTM) in London was host to a wonderful exploration of the rebozo shawl. In the 2014 exhibition 'Made in Mexico: The Rebozo in Art, Culture and Fashion', the FTM highlighted a shawl style made popular by the artist Frida Kahlo. Placing the shawl in a wider context, the exhibition considered how the rebozo has promoted Mexico throughout the world. This shawl not only is considered a traditional garment but also captures the essence of the country of origin and became known as a cultural emblem. As a source of inspiration, this exhibition provided a wealth of colour, texture and technique. Visitors were able to discover a wide variety of historical and contemporary examples of rebozo-shawl design.

Studying specific examples of shawls in museums, exhibitions and collections also reveals evidence of knitters customizing traditional designs. This can be an unexpected pattern placed within the shawl shape or an interesting new construction method. The following examples were encountered on a research visit to the KCG Collection that provided the opportunity to view knitted shawls and knitting publications and, most importantly, to talk to the knowledgeable archivists.

The Knitting and Crochet Guild Collection

A large number of fascinating shawl examples can be found in the KCG Collection. The Collection is located in Britannia Mills in Slaithwaite, UK, and is available to view by appointment. Many items are now digitized and can be viewed through the Guild's website, https://kcguild.org.uk.

The shawls in the KCG Collection provide an excellent insight into of some of the main styles of what are sometimes called traditional shawls. Many of the items in the Collection are donations from anonymous knitters or their families. The Guild accepts these donations as they are a record of items knitted in the home by knitters of many different skill levels. This section examines a selection of these shawls as examples to demonstrate how exploring the detailed construction of a shawl can inspire ideas for new shawl designs.

There are many ways to explore knitted items in a collection. These include handling the item carefully, usually wearing gloves, to examine joins, seams and edgings; photographing interesting details for a record of the visit; and sketching and drawing details. In particular, the technique of close-looking can be very helpful in this type of exploration. Art and dress historian Dr Ingrid E. Mida promotes drawing as a research tool in her recent book, *Reading Fashion in Art* (2020). In her lectures, most recently as part of a series of talks hosted by the Sartorial Society, she encourages this method of examining items. The close-looking approach is where the researcher uses drawing to visually explore the subject. It can lead to insights that would otherwise be missed by only taking a photograph:

> Drawing slows down and extends looking and, in the process of translating marks on to the page, the brain is able to discern additional information not otherwise seen in a single glance.

Details from shawls in the KCG Collection are described in this section, with reference to my own drawings and photographs of the items. Exploring these different shawl construction methods reveals many different ways to knit a shawl, especially focusing on examples of knitters adapting methods for their own particular designs.

Nineteenth-century rectangular shawl

One of the most straightforward ways to knit a shawl is to make a rectangle by casting on a number of stitches, knitting until the desired length is reached and then casting off the stitches. The effect of pattern placement and shawl construction within rectangles is beautifully illustrated through examples in the Collection.

An example of a hand-knitted nineteenth-century

Detail from nineteenth-century rectangular shawl, KCG Collection (2020.000.0030).

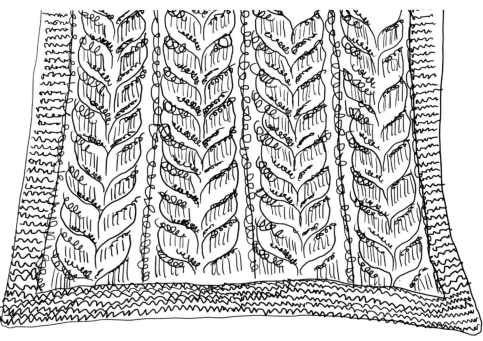

Sketch of nineteenth-century rectangular shawl from the KCG Collection.

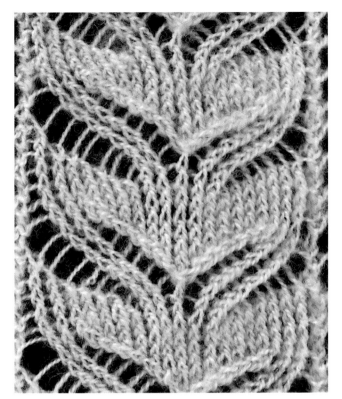

Pattern detail from nineteenth-century rectangular shawl, KCG Collection (2020.000.0030).

Sketch of detail from nineteenth-century rectangular shawl from the KCG Collection.

stole is this rectangular shawl knitted in a delicate lightweight cream wool yarn. The garter-stitch edgings have been knitted at the same time as the central pattern. Several rows of garter stitch have been worked before the main stitch pattern starts. Garter-stitch side borders, a few stitches wide, are worked at the beginning and end of each row. This simple border contrasts beautifully with the interlocking-leaf design knitted in the central panel.

An overall sketch of the stole and the stitch patterns helps to provide the starting point for a close exploration of the design. Drawing the delicate detail of the pattern shows how a long series of pattern repeats can be used as an elegant design feature. In this case, the same leaf motifs are repeated over the width and length of the shawl, creating unity in the design. Each leaf is formed with a series of eyelets. The curving lines of the motif contrast with long lines of eyelets running the full length of the rectangular shawl.

This shawl is an excellent example of the principles of creating a rectangular shawl. There is a border pattern that begins at the cast-on edge and runs up both sides of the shawl. The border appears to be knitted at the same time as the pattern. The knitter has calculated the number of stitches needed for the pattern repeats, added those needed for the two side borders, and then cast on this number of stitches. The choice of yarn has an effect on the pattern: knitted in a pure-wool yarn, the stitch-pattern structure is clearly visible.

Mirror-imaged rectangular shawl

Another rectangular-shawl example from the Collection shows several traditional construction techniques, including an intriguing mirror-imaged stitch pattern. This fine shawl has been knitted in Jamieson and Smith 1-ply (singles) cobweb-weight yarn. Close-looking reveals that this shawl is knitted from the centre outwards, with a border added after the rectangles were completed.

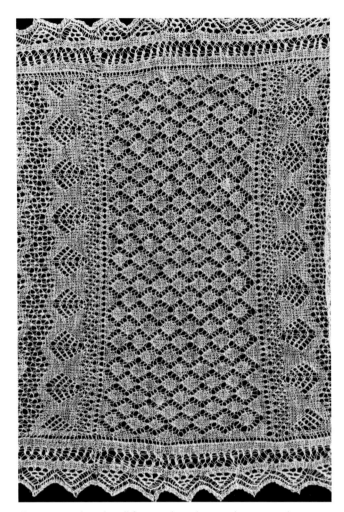

Centre-section detail from mirror-imaged rectangular shawl, KCG Collection (1998.071.0010).

Sketch of centre section of mirror-imaged rectangular shawl from the KCG Collection.

A provisional cast-on is the starting point for the first rectangle. After this rectangle is completed, the stitches from the provisional cast-on are unravelled. The revealed stitches are most likely picked up and used as the starting point for the second rectangle. Alternatively, a second matching rectangle is knitted with a provisional cast-on and the two rectangles are later grafted together. Both of these techniques ensure a mirror-imaged pattern. The two sides are nearly identical. The only difference is the starting point for the second rectangle. The whole central panel is worked as part of one of the rectangles and the join is on one side of this panel. The stitch pattern can be viewed either way around. However, close inspection reveals the direction of the stitches and the location of the join.

To complete this rectangular shawl, an outer border has been added around the whole shawl shape. Stitches were cast on for the border, and it was most likely attached as it was worked. To do this, the last stitch of every right-side row was knitted together with a loop from the edge of the shawl. Again, to create a seamless join, the border cast-on can be a provisional version. When the border is completed, the final stitches are grafted together with the cast-on stitches themselves or, if a provisional cast-on has been used, with the revealed live stitches at the cast-on end of the border.

Close-looking through sketching and drawing helps to reveal many details that are not immediately apparent. The sketches are made on different scales,

Sketch of detail from mirror-imaged rectangular shawl from the KCG Collection.

pattern placement and construction order are key to the appearance of the final shawl design.

Construction methods can be explored further in books. An excellent resource is *Heirloom Knitting* by Sharon Miller, published in 2002, a copy of which is held in the KCG Publications Collection. In her book, Sharon Miller provides beautiful illustrations of many Shetland-shawl construction methods. She includes ways to construct rectangles, squares, triangles and circles. The steps involved show how knitters use a combination of inherited traditional techniques combined with their own creativity to design shawls that are passed down through families over the years. The merging of individuality with tradition has resulted in truly original ideas.

from an overall plan of pattern placement to detail of the eyelets. Through these sketches, the direction of the stitch pattern becomes clear, and the joins between the sections of this fine shawl are a joy to observe. This stunning shawl is clearly the work of a master knitter.

The techniques used throughout this spectacular shawl demonstrate that shawl shapes can be made up of many components. From the mirror-imaged pattern to the order of construction, this shawl shows that there are many different ways to construct rectangle shapes and to place stitch patterns within these rectangles. The addition of the border after the centre was completed in the second example contrasts with the first shawl example, where the border was knitted at the same time as the central pattern. Decisions on

Centre-section detail from square shawl, KCG Collection (2002.065.0009).

Sketch of centre section of square shawl from the KCG Collection.

Square shawl

A square shawl can be constructed in a similar way to a rectangle, with stitches being cast on for the full width, rows being worked until the sides are the same length as that of the cast-on edge and then casting off to complete the shape. This fine-gauge square shawl in the Collection demonstrates a different construction technique; it is worked from the centre of the shawl outwards. There are four lines of increases, and the initial centre increase pattern has been used as a decorative feature, creating a beautiful flower motif.

This central pattern has rotational symmetry, with each of the four flower-petal panels being worked in the same way. The pattern contrasts beautifully with the outer-panel patterns. The long lines of eyelets that create the square shape begin within this motif and extend to the four corners.

Circular shawl

It can be seen from the previous examples that there are many different ways to knit shawl shapes. The KCG Collection features several variations on circular shawls, including one that demonstrates a wonderful swirl effect. Similar to the previous square-shawl example, this circular shawl is worked from the centre outwards. This knitter has also started the shawl with a distinctive decorative-centre increase section. In this case, the centre is worked in stocking stitch, contrasting with the main-panel pattern. To create a circular shape, there are seven increase lines radiating outwards for the centre panel. The decorative increase lines are formed of eyelets, and they spiral outwards towards the outer border. In contrast to the straight lines of increase in the square-shawl example, these increase lines appear

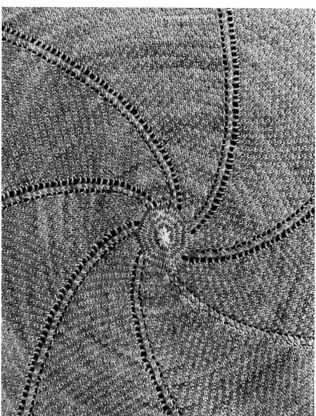

Detail of circular shawl, KCG Collection (2012.000.0054).

Sketch of circular shawl from the KCG Collection.

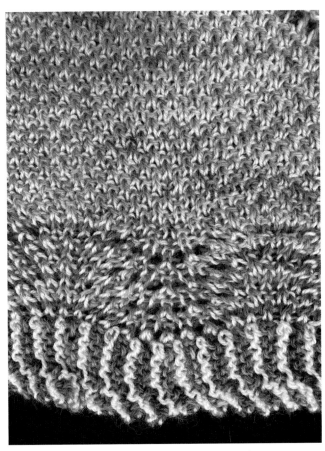

Edging detail from circular shawl, KCG Collection (2012.000.0054).

to move. This is achieved by working the increase one stitch after the position of the increase of the previous increase round.

The use of a variegated yarn, with multiple shades, in combination with a single-shade cream yarn, creates a lovely marl effect within the stitch pattern. The stripes of the colours are readily apparent within the stocking-stitch centre. These subtle stripes of colour become blurred within the main-shawl panels.

The shawl is completed with two border patterns; one is knitted as part of the main-shawl body and a second one is added around the entire outer circumference. The first border is worked in an old-shale or chevron pattern, in the round. Once this first border pattern is complete, a small number of stitches are cast on and a striped garter-stitch border is worked lengthwise. One stitch at the end of every right-side row is knitted together with a live stitch from the outer edge of the shawl. This border has been worked in stripes,

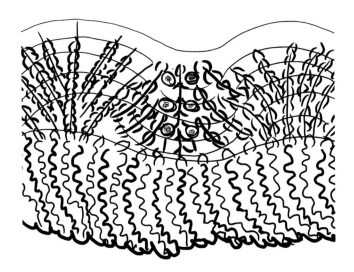

Sketch of edging from circular shawl from the KCG Collection.

using the same yarn shades as used for the main-shawl body. It creates a beautiful contrast to the main-shawl stitch patterns, with the stripes at right angles to the main-shawl colour stripes.

The interaction between the edging and the main shawl is shown in the sketch of the spiral-shawl border. A lovely scalloped edge has been formed by working the knitted-on edging after the chevron pattern. The increases and decreases of the chevrons cause the garter-stitch edge to undulate.

These fascinating examples from the KCG Collection demonstrate just a few of the myriad techniques that can be used to create a variety of different shawl shapes. They also demonstrate that knitters have always adapted and refined their work to suit the project and their own strengths. An appreciation of the shawls and the people who created them adds context to new designs.

Fashion Trends and Shawl Design

Fashion trends have a profound effect on accessories of all kinds, and shawls are no exception. Looking at historical and contemporary fashion trends can put designs into context and stimulate new ideas for shawls. For example, as dress silhouettes evolved to include wide skirts in the eighteenth and nineteenth centuries, shawl sizes increased in scale to be displayed over this framework. Shawls, such as the paisley shawl, have in turn influenced garments. In this case, after the fashion for this style of shawl began to wane, paisley shawls were remade as garments, with the distinctive patterning appearing on clothing of all kinds. The dialogue between accessories and fashion is ongoing. Importantly, accessories are often the more accessible and affordable part of high-fashion catwalk collections.

Engraving from Journal des Dames et des Modes, Costume Parisien, *25 Octobre 1809, Rijksmuseum Collection (http://hdl.handle.net/10934/RM0001.COLLECT.487455).*

Shawl, anonymous, c.1800–1825, Rijksmuseum Collection (http://hdl.handle.net/10934/RM0001.COLLECT.28406).

Illustration from La Mode, *25 September 1835, Pl.472: Chapeau de pail de rim, Georges Jaque Gatine, after Louis Marie Lanté, 1835 (http://hdl.handle.net/10934/RM0001. COLLECT.488615).*

Online museum collections, such as those of the Rijksmuseum, the Netherlands, can provide an excellent visual timeline of changing styles through art and design illustrations. Searching and browsing beautiful images provides an overview of shawl shapes and shawl patterns and reveals how they have changed over time. Beautiful illustrations from the *Mode de Paris* magazine series, courtesy of the Rijksmuseum, show how the silhouette of the prevailing fashion had an effect on shawls, as their shape and style changed to complement the most popular dress fashions.

Long, draping shawls could be worn with narrow column dresses or spread out over wide skirts. In particular, fashionable dress provided the perfect backdrop for the enormous paisley shawls of the nineteenth century. Large square shawls could be worn in the 'turn-over' style, with detailed pattern placed at opposite corners, as shown in the accompanying illustrations. The top corner was turned over to show a complementary pattern, matching the lower corner, and the shawl was draped around the shoulders with the two outer points held at the front.

Original Kashmir shawls were imported into Great Britain by the British East India Company. These extremely expensive shawls were in great demand. To satisfy this demand, weavers in the main production centres of Norwich, Edinburgh and Paisley produced more-affordable versions. The shawls made in Pais-

Imitation Kashmir shawl, Great Britain, anonymous, c.1815–1825, Rijksmuseum Collection (http://hdl.handle.net/10934/RM0001.COLLECT.28269).

Dolman, made out of a paisley shawl, anonymous, c.1880–1885 (http://hdl.handle.net/10934/RM0001.COLLECT.12230).

ley became the most prominent, and this style is still known as paisley pattern today.

The accompanying 1835 illustration is a lovely example of the importance of pattern placement. As the long rectangular shawl is worn draped around the shoulders, the ends of the shawl are on full display, meaning that the patterning at the two ends of the shawl is the most crucial. The imitation Kashmir shawl example shows how the stunning paisley patterns are placed only at the end of the shawl. The rest of the shawl consists of beautiful silk in a bold shade of red, with no visible patterning. As imitation Kashmir shawls became more widely available and more affordable, the original form became less desirable as a status symbol. Many shawls were cut up and remade into new garments such as capes, jackets and dolmans, as shown.

Today, luxury fashion houses frequently make use of their extensive archive material, releasing design updates for accessories. As the products of luxury fashion brands, a shawl, wrap or scarf can be an afford-able accessory that is more widely available than other exclusive items of clothing. Luxury fibres such as cashmere and silk are frequently used to create luxury scarves and shawls.

As a prime example, Italian fashion company Missoni have a large design archive. As well as developing new designs for garments and accessories, the company release design updates that pay homage to the originals. The many colours used within Missoni zigzag patterns are intrinsic to the brand. The combination of distinctive colours, alongside a wide selection of luxury fibres, defines the Missoni image.

A recent Burberry collection featured monogrammed blanket-size shawls as a variation on the poncho. As well as the placement of the distinctive Burberry check patterns on a large scale, the high-quality fibre used for the blankets was critical. The Burberry check is also used on a smaller scale on silk scarves, bags and other accessories.

As well as featuring high-quality fibre and distinctive design, the opportunity to customize an accessory is an important development. An innovative approach to customized knitwear was developed in 2014 by a company called Knyttan, now known as Unmade. Using a console in the design-studio showroom located at Somerset House in London, customers were able to alter one of several designs to suit their own specifications. By running a finger or a stylus across a set of prepared patterns, the design could be altered in a number of ways. For example, a houndstooth check could be broken up, to disrupt the pattern. This personalized pattern was then realized through a customized industrial knitting machine, producing a bespoke, high-quality knitted scarf. This whole process, including the scarf being knitted, could be viewed by visitors to the studio.

This early collaboration, including the disrupted houndstooth scarf, was with the design studio Moniker. Unmade went on to work with a number of fashion companies and designers, including developing the means for customers to create personal versions of Christopher Raeburn's Spring Summer 2016 catwalk sweaters.

The company now consults with manufacturers to create products that can be customized, using software called UnmadeOS. Knitwear manufacturer Johnstons of Elgin became Unmade's first manufacturing partner in 2017 as a response to the challenges of shifting from large production runs to smaller-scale, more-bespoke work:

> The Unmade order management system enables unique knitwear to be produced at an industrial scale for the same cost as mass production.

A recent client is the sportswear company New Balance:

> New Balance and Unmade have come together to combine manufacturing heritage with digital technology to create a new customisation experience for consumers, allowing them to create their own knitted shoe upper with a choice of graphics, colour and text, creating an entirely bespoke product.

By directly interacting with the knitting pattern for the shoe, a customer can create a unique version. There are currently six colourways and three patterns available for the customer to manipulate.

This innovative technology shows that there is demand from consumers to customize and personalize knitwear. The example of Unmade relates to customized knitting at industrial-scale production. In smaller-scale hand-knitting projects, the focus is on individual knitters and the projects on their knitting needles. In the world of hand knitting, a large number of beautiful shawl patterns are regularly published through knitting magazines, books and online platforms. These shawls are designed by a wide variety of designers working in very different ways. From in-house design teams at large yarn companies to independent designers, there are hand-knitting shawl patterns available to suit everyone's taste and ability. Although the world of fashion has enormous influence over shape, colour and style, it is the highly creative individual designers who are leading the way forward through experimentation and bold design development.

Hand-knitting design can therefore be considered the ultimate in design customization. By building on tradition, embracing innovation and developing our own original designs, we can all create knitted shawls that are truly unique.

CHAPTER 2

YARN, TOOLS AND TECHNIQUES

Yarn

Choosing yarn for making shawls can be very personal or can be determined by the pattern that a knitter wishes to follow. A shawl is the perfect way to showcase a beautiful yarn created as a one-off by a talented independent dyer. The yarn may be selected to be worn with specific clothing or to be a gift for a particular person. Some shawl styles have a distinct relationship with very specific fibres and are even defined by the fibre. Examples include Shetland shawls and Kashmir/cashmere shawls.

Altering the yarn weight, fibre or colour can have a dramatic effect on scale, colour balance and pattern. Shawl patterns are in general very versatile. Using a lighter-weight yarn can mean that a smaller shawl results that can take longer to knit. A heavier weight of yarn will generally result in a larger shawl that could require a larger quantity of yarn. Two knitters knitting the same pattern but with different yarns will create two very different shawls. Experimentation through knitting swatches is one of the best ways to work out what works with a specific pattern and, most importantly, what you like best.

In this book, the yarns for projects have been chosen in the same way that the stitch patterns are developed.

OPPOSITE: Close-up of Las Setas Shawl, showing the pattern detail of short-row shaping used between the segments (dark-blue inserts) and within each individual segment (each side of eyelet pattern).

This method begins by considering the effects to be created, followed by choosing a yarn that best meets these criteria; a great example is the Open Doors Shawl (*see* Chapter 12). The yarn perfectly matches the inspirational source in both the fibre content and the colourway. The silk and bamboo content of the chosen

Security gates by John Creed, Kelvingrove Art Gallery and Museum, Glasgow, UK.

Irish Artisan Yarn merino–bamboo–silk blend used for knitting the Open Doors Shawl.

Open Doors Shawl knitted with Irish Artisan Yarn.

Irish Artisan Yarn provides a metallic sheen inspired by John Creed's stunning metal security gates at the Kelvingrove Art Gallery and Museum in Glasgow. The delicately placed hand-dyed colours pick up on the hints of red and green reflected in the steel-grey doors. In each project in this book, there is an explanation of how the yarn choice was made to fulfil the individual criteria considered.

Yarn and the design process

Once an inspirational source has been determined, the experimentation stage can begin. Trying out a wide variety of yarn fibres and weights increases the design potential and may result in some exciting new applications. Using different yarn weights and fibres to enhance your shawl design is one of the most straightforward ways to create new variations.

The main elements to consider include the appearance of any stitch pattern in the shawl design. A laceweight yarn will result in a lightweight, translucent shawl. A loosely spun aran-weight yarn will create a warm, dense knitted fabric. However, this depends on the complexity of the stitch pattern. An openwork lace design can be light and airy, whereas a tightly cabled pattern may appear too dense. In this latter case, the knitted fabric could detract from the pattern rather than enhancing it. With so many options, it is useful to compare some of the main yarn weights and fibres. Keeping this comparison in mind when making other design decisions can really help to unify individual shawl-design elements.

Without doubt, the best way to work out the best yarn for a stitch pattern is to knit a test swatch. This allows the design to be seen knitted up in the chosen yarn and allows the designer to modify the pattern to suit that yarn. A basic test swatch may involve only a small number of pattern repeats. Additionally, adding the proposed edging stitches and the cast-on and cast-off borders will provide extremely useful information. If a knitter is planning to use a yarn other than the recommended yarn of a pattern, it is always worth taking the time to knit a test swatch. Sometimes, the way that the yarn behaves with the pattern specified is very unexpected!

In the design process, the next step would be to knit

a larger swatch that can then be used to calculate the tension. Sometimes these steps can be combined, but it is important to have the opportunity to experiment and play with the pattern before committing to the whole design. This is where an unexpected character of the pattern or a mistake can result in a whole new and original different design.

The swatches shown in the accompanying image illustrate the design developments for the Modernism Shawl (*see* Chapter 11). The initial samples were knitted in a different yarn to that of the final shawl pattern, to demonstrate an alternative effect. Experimenting with different yarns and shades in the early design stages opens up options and possibilities.

Yarn and swatching

Designs can always be customized and modified to suit both the knitter and the wearer of the shawl. An immediate impact on any design can be made by changing the weight or fibre of the yarn. As previously mentioned, the effect of altering either factor is best seen through knitting a sample swatch. To illustrate this process, the swatch examples throughout this book have been knitted with a variety of different fibres and yarn weights. Where a final pattern has been included, the yarn used may differ from that used for the experimental swatches. This is because trying out the pattern and shape in different yarns is essential to the decision-making process. Additionally, before writing any final pattern, a tension swatch is always knitted with the chosen yarn.

Although certain general principles apply, such as the number of stitches and rows in a tension sample, it is through swatching that the designer can see the impact of their choices. At this stage, designs can be amended and alterations made. There is nothing wrong with jumping straight into a pattern. However, especially if a change of yarn is made, taking time to explore the pattern with the chosen yarn is well worthwhile. For example, if the same pattern were to be knitted with a 4ply sock yarn and with an aran-weight roving yarn, the first point to note would be the change of scale. Each individual stitch in the aran-weight sample would appear larger than an individual stitch

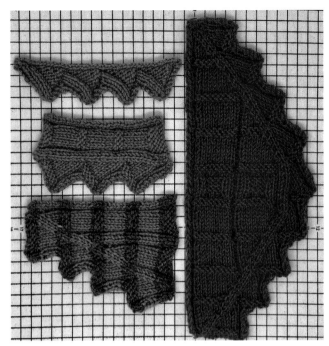

Swatches exploring edgings and borders for the Modernism Shawl.

in the 4ply sample. The stitch-pattern scale would also alter. A cable pattern worked in the sample would appear wider and bolder with the aran-weight yarn. In particular, the stitch definition may be clearer from the smooth twist of the 4ply yarn. These two yarn weights are very different in many ways. However, both could capture the essence of the design in their own way, through colour or fibre.

Making decisions about which yarn to choose can be helped by going back to the inspiration behind the design. What is the pattern about? Does the design work better on a larger or smaller scale? Which fibre would the wearer more enjoy wrapping around them? Which time of year is the knitting being done and in what weather is the shawl more likely to be worn?

Answers to all of these questions can help in making design decisions. Ultimately, it can just be a choice of using the yarn available to you and making it work in the best way possible. A yarn may benefit from being worked with a larger needle size than the ball band recommends. This can help with drape and opening up the pattern lines with a looser tension. Again, swatching will show whether or not this approach works. Look closely at your own knitted samples, and use some of the questions posed to determine and select your preferences.

Knitting a shawl swatch will also show the parts of the shawl that can be extended or reduced. This is particularly important where a variety of widths and lengths are to be provided. Not all shawl shapes suit all wearers, and providing the opportunity to customize a design can be really helpful to the knitter. Sometimes extending a shawl can be as straightforward as purchasing another ball or skein and knitting more pattern repeats. In other cases, more than one part of the shawl has to be extended to balance the shawl shape. Knitting a small version immediately shows where these adjustments can successfully be made.

Understanding shawl shapes can really help in this respect. Thinking of each section of a shawl as a distinct shape helps to break down the construction and show which section is best to add length or width to or to subtract it from. In Parts 2 and 3 of this book, a selection of shapes are looked at in detail, with instructions provided for each one. Placing your chosen pattern into a category of these different shapes can really help you to visualize how the overall shawl will look.

Planning a test swatch
This section concentrates on yarn choices and illustrates some of the properties of yarn through the knitting of small test swatches for comparison. However, whether the primary reason for creating a swatch is to test a new yarn or experiment with a stitch pattern, there are several general principles to take into account. Although swatch planning steps can be presented as a sequence, creative design is much more free-flowing. Sometimes, the idea for a border is the first step; other times, the yarn guides the whole design. Be flexible and willing to try new techniques and methods throughout.

Firstly, decide whether the swatch is an initial test swatch or, if the design is already more advanced, a tension swatch. The difference will be crucial to future calculations. If the design is in the early stages, the main purpose of the swatch is to try out new ideas with a particular yarn and to test different parts of the pattern. These types of swatches can be smaller and more experimental. However, even when experiment-ing with stitch patterns in the test yarn, make sure that there are enough repeats of the pattern to show the pattern progression within the swatch. For calculating actual stitches and rows of a final knitting pattern, the swatch must be large enough to allow accurate tension measurements to be taken.

Edging and border patterns will be considered in Chapter 3, but, for yarn-swatching purposes, some initial border decisions are required. Try to choose a swatch border pattern that helps with the pattern development. For example, consider using a garter-stitch border for the initial test swatch; this helps to focus the swatch on the yarn suitability for the main stitch pattern and can be changed for later swatches, if a different style of border is then selected. However, where the border pattern is a key component of the whole design, such as for the Modernism Shawl, it can help to begin with swatches for this section and then add the shawl shape at a later stage. This is demonstrated in early design swatches for the Modernism Shawl, pictured earlier.

Consider making more than one swatch to explore the chosen yarn, using a different needle size for each for working the same stitch pattern. This will help to check how the yarn drapes when knitted at different tensions. A good starting point is the recommended needle size on the yarn ball band.

Take notes when knitting a swatch, especially recording which needle size was used with which yarn. These notes will help when trying to reproduce the look and feel of the preferred version. Remember that it is acceptable to make changes at any stage. The idea of swatching is to help develop and refine a design, so that the end result is the best it can be. Try not to undo mistakes. Sometimes these errors lead to the most interesting designs!

Yarn information

A great deal of information can be gathered about a yarn before it even reaches the needles. Look at the ball band or label. Read information online and in magazines. Many independent yarn shops take great pride in sourcing very special yarns. They provide information and detail about the yarn producers to help customers to make decisions. Magazines often review yarns and provide summary notes. If using a hand-spun or hand-dyed yarn, talk to the spinner or dyer who has created the product. Yarn shows are a great place to gather information and to find out about the source of the fibre and the way that the yarn has been processed. Yarn is usually sold in balls or skeins; when purchasing yarn in skeins, the yarn will require winding into cakes before being knitted.

Key information to look for when deciding on the yarn to use for a shawl includes the following:

- the weight of the ball, hank or skein in grams or ounces
- the specific fibre content (especially important for a blended yarn, where the actual proportions of the different fibres may have an impact on the final knitted fabric)
- the metreage or yardage stated, which indicates the length of the yarn in the ball, hank or skein and helps to determine how much yarn will be needed for a project

- the standard tension and knitting-needle size to achieve the recommended tension. A knitter may need to adjust needle size for several reasons. Tension is usually given for stocking stitch. To match this tension, you may need to go up or down a needle size or half size (or more). Additionally, a different needle size may better suit the specific stitch pattern. A pattern with a high density of twists and cables may have a more even tension when worked on larger needles.
- the international symbols for garment care. This cleaning and pressing information is always listed and is essential to consider when blocking or dressing any knitting, whether it is a swatch or a finished item.
- the shade name and number and the dye-lot code. For a project involving multiple balls or skeins of yarn, it is important to have all of balls being from the same dye lot, as otherwise subtle but unwanted colour variations can show up in the finished knitting.

Yarn categories

Category name	Common label names (UK, USA, AUS and NZ)	Stocking-stitch tension per 10cm/4in	Recommended needle size
Lace	Lace; baby; cobweb; thread; 2ply; 3ply	33–40 sts	1.5–2.25mm (000–1 US)
4ply (light)	Super fine; sock; light fingering; baby; 3ply; 4ply	27–32 sts	2.25–3.25mm (1–3 US)
4ply	Fine; sport; fingering; baby; sock; 4ply; 5ply	23–26 sts	3.25–3.75mm (3–5 US)
DK	DK (double-knitting); light worsted; sport; 8ply	21–24 sts	3.75–4.5mm (5–7 US)
Aran	Aran; medium; worsted; 10ply	16–20 sts	4.5–5.5mm (7–9 US)
Chunky	Chunky; bulky; 10–12ply	12–15 sts	5.5–8mm (9–11 US)
Super chunky	Super chunky; super bulky; roving; 14–16ply	7–11 sts	8–12.75mm (11–17 US)

Table of yarn categories used throughout this book, including label names commonly used in the UK, US, Australia and New Zealand to describe yarns. This list is intended as a guide to help with design choices and is not a complete list.

Yarn weight

The best way to determine the preferred yarn weight for a project is to knit a small swatch. In this case, yarn weight refers to the thickness of a fibre strand rather than the weight of a skein or ball. For shawl design, a yarn can frequently be knitted with a larger needle size than that recommended on the ball band to create beautiful drape. Not all yarns are suitable for this, and, again, the best way to check is to test this approach by working a small swatch.

The main points to consider are how yarn weight affects the scale of the patterning and the overall size of the shape. For example, using a lace-weight yarn and the recommended needle size results in small-scale eyelets on a tiny shape. As the needle size is increased, the relative size of the eyelets increases and the overall size of the shape becomes larger. However, the individual stitch size has also increased, and, if the needle size is too large, the knitted fabric can become unstable. Ultimately, this can result in the overall shawl shape becoming distorted. Working with a larger-than-specified needle size can also help to increase the drape of the knitted fabric. Some yarns drape beautifully when knitted loosely, but others will distort. Again, these limitations can be tested with a small sample swatch before embarking on the larger project.

Yarn fibre

Choosing the appropriate fibre of the yarn for a shawl project is just as important as the yarn weight and colour. Linking the fibre choice to the inspiration for the project can help to narrow down the options. For example, a precise, embossed stitch pattern may look best worked in a pure-wool yarn with great stitch definition. However, a colour-gradient project may be best represented by using a mohair-based yarn, as the fibres will blur the progression of colours and create a more seamless transition of colour changes. Of course, combining these two elements may create the most interesting pattern of all! Experimenting within a test swatch will show how fibre influences the design.

As well as considering a particular fibre for a project, many knitting yarns are a blend of fibres. These yarns provide the best characteristics from more than one fibre in the form of a single yarn. For example, the Irish Artisan Yarn hand-dyed yarn used for the Open Doors Shawl (see Chapter 12) combines merino wool, bamboo and silk. This blend results in a yarn that has the excellent stitch definition associated with wool fibre, but both the silk and bamboo fibres bring a sheen and a softness to the blend. Each individual project will have its own requirements that will suit different fibre blends.

Fibre can also determine the texture of the knitted fabric. A loosely spun slub yarn can distort the stitch definition and create interesting pattern effects. A tightly spun fibre can create great stitch definition.

Working on shawl projects creates the ideal opportunity to play and experiment with yarns and fibres. Using one or two skeins of an expensive yarn can create a beautiful shawl, whereas the quantity required would be prohibitively expensive for making a garment.

Yarn style

The style of a yarn is distinct from its fibre or its weight and is sometimes more closely linked to the way that the yarn has been spun. This aspect must be considered carefully, as it can have a profound effect on pattern and shape. Yarn styles range from smooth yarns spun from filament fibres to those with more textured appearances. Common examples include bouclé, brushed and slub yarns.

Slub yarns have an uneven thickness with alternating sections of tight and loose spinning. The stitches of any pattern knitted in the slub yarn will vary in thickness, depending on which part of the yarn is used to produce particular stitches. The shawl edges will be more varied, so this style of yarn should be avoided if precise, straight-edged shapes are required. However, for a bold-and-chunky shawl design or to deliberately distort a pattern, use of a slub yarn would be ideal.

A superwash merino yarn has a smooth appearance and is of the same diameter throughout the length of the whole ball of yarn. As a result, this gives an even texture throughout a whole cable braid; the size of the stitches and the lines of knitting are completely consistent throughout.

It is also possible to create your own custom blends of yarn styles by combining two or more yarns made with different fibres. For example, a lace-weight mohair blend yarn could be held and knitted together with a fine silk yarn, to create a custom style of knitted fabric. The shades of the combined yarns could be matching, or one yarn shade could provide a contrast to the other. There are many exciting possibilities, and, to help make decisions about yarn style, use the original inspirational source as your guide.

Tools

Knitting needles

The best size of knitting needles for a shawl project depends on a combination of the effect that the knitter wishes to create and the tension required for the knitted fabric. The best style of needle to use is influenced by the largest number of stitches that will be worked and, most importantly, the knitter's preference. For example, circular needles can be used for working a circular centre-out shawl and can also be used to knit flat projects back and forth. The most important factor is that the choice of needles should give the knitter the freedom to relax and enjoy the project, while allowing plenty of room for all of the stitches to be held securely on the needles of choice.

Needle types
Straight, single-pointed needles are produced in pairs in a variety of lengths and can be used only for flat knitting. The preferable length is determined by how the knitter holds their work. For example, a longer length is needed to tuck one end of a needle under one arm; a shorter length suffices if the needle is to be held in a similar way to a pen.

Circular needles can be used for flat or circular knitting and consist of two very short needles connected by a strong flexible cord or wire. The needles can be interchangeable, so that different lengths of cord or wire can be used, depending on the requirements of the project.

Double-pointed needles (dpns) are made as sets of four or five needles and are usually used for circular knitting. If used with a removable 'stop' at one end, they can also be used for flat knitting.

Knitting needles are manufactured in a wide variety of different materials. Examples of commonly available materials include bamboo, wood (such as birch, rosewood and olive), carbon fibre, aluminium, steel and plastic. Using the same size of needles but made of a different material can result in different stitch tensions. It is therefore important to use the same type of needles throughout the working of each swatch, design and project.

Needle sizes
There is freedom to experiment with knitting-needle sizes in shawl design. Moving to a size larger than the ball-band recommended needle can create beautiful drape and a translucent effect in the knitted fabric. An openwork pattern can be enhanced with use of a larger needle size, with the individual stitches and holes becoming larger. However, this is not always a satisfactory result. Stitches can become too loose, and the knitted fabric can more easily distort. A test swatch can show the effect of changing needle size. Blocking or dressing the swatch and final shawl is essential to set the pattern and stabilize the knitting.

After the desired combination of yarn and needle size has been established, accurate tension measurements can be taken. If a different yarn is then used to knit the final version of the shawl, it is very important that the tension matches that of the original, otherwise the dimensions of the finished shawl will not be the same as of the sample. This may not matter if the discrepancies are small. However, it is very important to be aware of differences that may occur. If there are more stitches than stated in the tension measurements, in other words, the tension is tighter, then the final shawl will be smaller. In contrast, if there are fewer stitches than the established tension, or a looser tension, then the shawl will be larger. This may or may not matter. However, the stitch pattern may look completely different when worked in a different yarn at a different tension, and this may cause the greatest disappointment. I always recommend knitting a tension swatch with the selected yarn and needles, as this will give you an idea of how the end result will look, before committing to the whole project.

Metric	UK	US
2mm	14	0
2.25mm	13	0
2.5mm	–	–
2.75mm	12	2
3mm	11	–
3.25mm	10	3
3.5mm	–	4
3.75mm	9	5
4mm	8	6
4.5mm	7	7
5mm	6	8
5.5mm	5	9
6mm	4	10
6.5mm	3	10½
7mm	2	–
7.5mm	1	–
8mm	0	11
9mm	00	13
10mm	000	15
12mm	–	17
16mm	–	19
19mm	–	35
25mm	–	50

Table of common knitting-needle size equivalents.

Additional knitting equipment

Blocking board

All of the knitted samples shown in this book have been blocked before being photographed. The blocking process is essential to relax the knitted stitches and show a design at its best. There are many different blocking surfaces available, from using a spare piece of carpet covered with a clean cloth to using a custom-sized foam mat.

There are some important elements to consider when constructing a blocking board. The board should enable the safe pinning out of the knitting without any other surface being pierced unintentionally. The surface must be able to tolerate the heat and steam of an iron. If the knitting is to be wet blocked by soaking, the surface must be able to tolerate water without any colour running into the work or damage occurring to the underlying surface. My own blocking board consists of a sturdy backing covered with ironing-board cushioning fabric and also an ironing-board cover for heat protection. This cover also has straight-line and measurement markings, which can be used to help to align the edges of knitted samples.

Blocking wires

Blocking can completely transform a shawl from a crumpled knitted fabric to a truly magical flat shape. Extending the cast-off points on a top-down shawl adds depth and creates delicate features. The points can be pinned out individually, or blocking wires can be threaded through the tips and the whole series of points then be extended to the same extent in one go. T-pins are extremely useful for this, as they can either tension the blocking wires into the desired curve or line or be used for fixing individual points of the shawl. Try to maintain the intended design lines, and make sure that all of the points are blocked to the same depth.

Scales

A set of digital scales is extremely useful for shawl projects. They are used to calculate and keep track of yarn amounts available for the whole shawl and sections of the shawl. It is always worth checking the actual weight of a ball of yarn before beginning any project, as it may be slightly more or less than is stated on the ball band.

Triangular swatch pinned out to dry on a blocking board.

Cable needles

An essential tool for working some cable patterns, cable needles are produced in a wide variety of materials and thicknesses. The most important factor to consider when choosing a cable needle is that it is comfortable to work with. This will also be affected by the weight of the yarn and the fibre being used. A highly polished cable needle will be very helpful with a textured yarn, but it may be challenging to hold on to stitches worked in a smooth cotton yarn, for example. In some cases, it may be more efficient to work smaller cable manoeuvres without a cable needle. This can be done by manipulating the live stitches and rearranging them off of the needles before knitting them in the correct order. For larger cable manipulations, a notched cable needle, with an indentation in the centre of its length, can help with holding on to the stitches.

Charting software

The charts present throughout this book have been created by using the excellent software programme Stitchmastery. The ability to produce stitch patterns in this format is extremely helpful in both the design-development and pattern-writing stages of shawl design. An alternative is to use either graph paper, of normal 'real' squares, or knitter's graph paper, for which the tension of the yarn and needles to be used is reflected in the size of the squares (which are usually actually rectangles).

Darning needles

A darning needle with a large eye and blunt point is used for sewing in the ends of yarn after blocking. The blunt point helps to avoid splitting the yarn unintentionally when the needle moves through the knitted fabric. For very chunky, thick or textured yarns, a plastic needle with a large looped eye is a useful alternative to an inflexible metal needle.

Pins

Glass-head pins are generally heat-resistant and are very useful to use during finishing processes. Points of a shawl can be pinned into precise shapes by using multiple pins.

T-pins are also used during finishing and are often used alongside blocking wires. The long length of the T-pin allows it to be placed at an angle, which is especially helpful when fixing a long length of blocking wire into place.

Safety pins are extremely versatile and can be used to hold sections of knitting in place during any sewing-up step. They can be used as removable stitch markers and, when attached to an individual stitch, can help to mark a mistake for correcting on a subsequent row.

Stitch holders

Stitch holders are used to keep live stitches from unravelling while another part of the knitting is being worked. They are commonly made of metal or plastic. A spare needle can also be used to temporarily hold stitches.

Stitch markers

Stitch markers can be used in a variety of ways. They show the knitter where a specific action must occur within a row. This action may be an increase, a decrease or a change in stitch pattern. The marker can also help within a complex repeat pattern, by indicating the performance of the same action over several rows with different numbers of stitches. For example, the instruction 'work to marker' allows more complicated instructions relevant for different numbers of stitches to be combined into one instruction instead. Once a knitter is comfortable with the pattern repeats, the stitch marker can be removed.

Stitch markers can be functional or decorative and made from a wide variety of materials, including a simple loop of yarn. This example from Mrs Gaugain's *The Lady's Workbook* (1842) involves using a piece of thread as a marker. In her receipt for a 'Handsome Triangular Knit Shawl', Mrs Gaugain includes the following pattern note (p.87):

> Note – It would be well to tie a piece of coloured wool to mark the middle of the Shawl, until you get into the mode of working it; as you may perceive, by what you have already worked, this Shawl is formed by increasing a stitch after the first two stitches, and before and after the four middle stitches; and again before the last two stitches.

Tape measure

The type of measure used can vary from a flexible tape to a hard plastic ruler. The most important consideration is to be consistent with the measuring units, working in either centimetres or inches throughout.

Yarn winder and swift

If yarn is purchased in skeins, it can be very helpful to use a yarn winder and a swift to wind the yarn into cakes or balls. Using the two tools together produces cakes with evenly tensioned yarn. Alternatively, the back of a chair holds a skein very securely, and a ball can be wound by hand.

Techniques

Shawl patterns provide an excellent opportunity to explore new stitch patterns and knitting methods. A shawl pattern can focus on just one technique or be a sampler for a wide variety of different methods. While there are new ideas for stitch patterns proposed throughout, a selection of general techniques referred to within this book are described in this section.

Increasing and decreasing

As well as forming the basis for many stitch patterns, increasing and decreasing techniques are used to create individual shawl shapes. Before beginning to work on a design, it is essential to review the types of increases and decreases that could be used. Different methods of increasing and decreasing can be decorative or integral to altering the stitch count, or both.

Increasing

Increases are worked to add stitches in order to widen a shawl shape. These stitches can be added at the beginning, end or centre of a row or be distributed across a row, depending on the shape to be formed. The precise placement of increases will be looked at within the shawl-shape chapters (*see* Part 2). This section describes the main types of increase methods and considers their advantages and disadvantages.

Open or closed increases change the way that a knitted fabric looks and behaves. An open increase is where a new stitch is formed with a loop of yarn. These types of increase stitches are often referred to by one of the following terms:

yb: yarn back (forming a loop over the right-hand needle, when the next stitch is to be a purl stitch)
yfd: yarn forward (forming a loop over the right-hand needle, when the next stitch is to be a knit stitch)
yo: yarn over – take the yarn over the right-hand needle from front to back. This is the most commonly used open increase.
yob: yarn over backwards – take the yarn over the

right-hand needle from back to front (for more information about this increase, *see* the special abbreviation in the pattern section of Chapter 12)

yrn: yarn round needle – take the yarn around the right-hand needle

In most modern patterns, all yarn overs are written as 'yo', with the understanding that the knitter will recognize that there are different ways of working this increase and use the appropriate one.

A closed increase is worked without a loop and is usually referred to by one the following terms:

kfb: knit front and back – knit into the front and then the back of the next stitch on the left-hand needle, then allow this knitted-into stitch to slip off of the left-hand needle point (1st inc'd)

m1: make one (also known as m1l) – make 1 stitch by bringing the tip of the left-hand needle from front to back under the strand of yarn running between the stitches sitting closest to the tips of the left- and right-hand needles and then knitting through the back of this loop (1st inc'd)

m1p: make one purlwise – make 1 stitch purlwise by bringing the tip of the left-hand needle from front to back under the strand of yarn running between the stitches sitting closest to the tips of the left- and right-hand needles and then purling through the back of this loop (1st inc'd)

pfb: purl front and back – purl into the front and then the back of the next stitch on the left-hand needle, then allow this purled-into stitch to slip off of the left-hand needle point (1st inc'd)

The preferred increase method will depend on the rest of the stitch pattern. Yarn-over increases fit perfectly with an openwork lace design, but they may look out of place if there are no other eyelets in the pattern. Closed increases can sometimes make the knitted fabric too dense and the surrounding stitches spread less easily. Try out increase options within a test swatch before deciding on the best one for a project. The most important factor is to be consistent within the pattern,

Pattern placement for the Cardiff Bay Shawl.

as this helps to avoid confusion and creates a consistent design.

The Cardiff Bay Shawl (*see* Chapter 10) has open yarn-over increases along the top edge and down the central spine. These increases were chosen as they match the openwork stitch pattern of the main-shawl sections.

A further variation of a yarn-over increase is a looped-edge increase, where a yarn over is made before the first stitch of the row is worked. This is also used as a decorative outer border stitch. The advantage of a looped edge is that the increase is made at the beginning of every row, rather than only on right-side rows. The disadvantages are that a missed loop can affect the pattern placement and create an obvious gap on the edge of the shawl.

A double-yarn-over increase is where the yarn is wrapped around the right-hand needle twice, creating two new stitches. This double increase can be very useful within crescent shawl shapes, where the number of stitches increases at a faster rate than is achieved with a normal, single, yarn over.

Sometimes, a pattern does not specify the type of increase to be used, for example, in a vintage pattern. The knitter can select their own style of increase, remembering to be consistent and to try to match the style of the main stitch patterns.

Left- and right-leaning closed increases

Different shawl shapes will require increases to be made in a variety of locations. Where matching increases are made on each side of a central point, paired increases are the best option. Paired increases are a mirror image of each other in appearance.

The left- and right-leaning increases m1l and m1r are both made by lifting the strand or little bar of yarn running between the stitches sitting closest to the tips of the left- and right-hand needles and knitting into it. The difference in the way that the increase stitch leans is created by the direction in which the bar is lifted and worked. Using these two increase techniques – m1l and m1r – together creates paired increases that are in balance visually.

Decreasing

Decreases are worked to decrease the stitch count. Decreases can be used as part of a stitch pattern or to create a specific shawl shape. For example, modular-style shawl constructions using mitred-corner techniques use double decreases to create the square shape of the mitre. The precise use and placement of the decreases will be looked at in detail in Part 2.

Where two decreases are required at opposite ends of a row, they are often worked in matching pairs of k2tog (knit two stitches together) and ssk (slip two

stitches knitwise, one at a time, then knit the two slipped stitches together through the backs of their loops).

Paired decreases are used to shape the back of the neck of the Open Doors Shawl. The main stitch pattern continues to be worked as stitches are decreased. This means that partial repeats of the main pattern are required. During this process, the knitter makes on-going decisions about which parts of the stitch pattern to include or leave out. In the shawl pattern, the instructions include guidance for the knitter, including, for example, to knit a stitch that would have been included in a k2tog decrease and to purl a stitch that would have been in the position of a yob or yo increase.

The first stitch of the row

Edging patterns are explored in depth in Chapter 3; however, whichever pattern is used, from a few stitches to an elaborate design, the first stitch of each row can determine the neatness of the outer edges. As with all of the stitch patterns and projects in this book, the choice of edge stitch depends on the effect that you wish to create.

A slipped stitch worked at the beginning of every row provides a neat and decorative chain edge that can help to keep the shawl edges lying flat. However, there may be certain patterns where you wish to create a looser edge, especially if stitches will later be picked up along the edge for a border to be added after the shawl shape is completed. The best way to work out the appropriate approach required is to knit a small swatch. This will show which option works best with the chosen stitch pattern and shawl shape and according to individual preference.

The projects in the book generally have a slipped stitch worked at the beginning of every row. These slipped stitches vary in how they are worked between having the yarn at the back of the work and having the yarn at the front of the work when the stitch is slipped. For example, with the rib-pattern edging of the Open Doors Shawl, the right-side rows have the first stitch slipped with the yarn at the back of the work. For the wrong-side rows, the yarn is instead at the front of the work. This is because the first stitch of the right-side

Paired decreases are used for the back-of-neck shaping of the Open Doors Shawl.

The first stitch of every row has been slipped, forming a neat edge for the Open Doors Shawl.

The Cardiff Bay Shawl starts with a garter-stitch tab.

row is effectively a knit stitch, which has been already worked as a purl stitch at the end of the previous wrong-side row. The first stitch of the wrong-side rows is worked as a purl stitch, as it has already been worked as a knit stitch at the end of the previous right-side row.

As well as the decorative chain-stitch edge, another option for working the first stitch of each row is a knitted selvedge. A knitted selvedge is where the first stitch of every row is knitted. This technique is useful for where there is an adjacent stocking-stitch pattern and for an edge that will later have stitches picked up from it for a border to be worked after the shawl shape is completed. The disadvantage of this type of first stitch is that changes in tension can be very visible, and the first stitch may look loose.

Tabs

A tab is a small block of knitting that is used to fill in the gap that could otherwise be present at the top of a top-down shawl. Without this tab, a small dent appears in the knitted fabric, and, although the shawl is perfectly fine without the tab, using this technique creates a smooth edge across the top of the shawl, which many find more visually attractive.

The tab usually consists of three stitches that are knitted over eight to ten rows. Stitches are picked up along one long edge of the tab and then along the cast-on edge, making a total of eight or ten stitches, depending on the project. These stitches are the beginning point for the shawl pattern. Tabs are most commonly worked in garter stitch. However, they can also be worked in a different stitch pattern that suits the shawl project.

The Cardiff Bay Shawl begins with a garter-stitch tab: it is located at the top of the 'T' in the centre of the top edge of the shawl. The edging along the top of the shawl and the pattern for the central spine are both worked in garter stitch. This means that the tab bridges the gap between these elements of the shawl perfectly. It also provides a stable start to the increase pattern and allows the top edge to be blocked to a straight line. Full instructions on how to knit such a tab are provided in the pattern (*see* Chapter 10).

Picking up stitches

Stitches are required to be picked up for many different reasons. Working the garter-stitch tab described previously is one example. Multidirectional shawls require shawl sections to be worked at different angles. For the Riverside Shawl (*see* Chapter 9), stitches for the outer wings are picked up along the sides of the

Close-up of the right side of the edge of the Riverside Shawl where stitches are picked up for the shawl wings.

Close-up of the wrong side of the edge of the Riverside Shawl where stitches are picked up for the shawl wings.

central square. The wings are then worked lengthwise. The accompanying images show the right and wrong sides of these pick-up edges.

Modular shawls, worked using the mitred-corner technique, explained in Chapter 4, consist of multiple blocks of shapes. These can of course be sewn together after the knitting is completed. However, picking up stitches means having fewer seams to work later on.

Edging patterns can be added to a shawl by picking up all or part of the stitches and working the edging from this new set of stitches.

Always try the proposed techniques before working on the final shawl design. There is usually more than one way to achieve a desired effect, and test swatches are the way to work out and confirm the best approach for a particular project.

When picking up stitches along an edge consisting of rows, it is usual to have the right side of the work facing. The needle is inserted into the gaps between the outermost stitches of the rows and those stitches adjacent to them. In general, follow the 'three-for-two' rule, where approximately two stitches are picked up for every three rows. This will, though, depend on the tension of the knitted fabric. Try not to pull too tight or to leave loose stitches on the needle.

Short-row shaping

Adding short (or partial) rows to knitting is an extremely useful technique. Partial rows can be used to create shapes, add depth and shape edgings. In this book, they are used for samples and patterns throughout the shape and the project chapters in many different ways.

For the Cardiff Bay Shawl (*see* Chapter 10), short-row shaping is worked around each of the three points of the triangle. The partial rows add extra depth to these selected areas and enhance the edging pattern by extending its points.

For the Las Setas Shawl (*see* Chapter 13), short rows are worked in two different ways. The first set creates the overall crescent shape of the shawl, by adding more rows to the outer section of the shawl. Short rows are also used decoratively along the inner edge of the shawl, with long, narrow sections being worked in a contrasting yarn shade.

When using short rows, a stitch is wrapped to avoid a gap remaining in the knitting where each short row is worked. This wrapping action is known as wrap and turn, 'w&t'. To wrap a stitch, knit to the stitch to be wrapped; slip the next stitch purlwise; take the yarn to the back of the work; slip the slipped stitch back to the left-hand needle purlwise without working it; take the yarn to the front of the work; and turn the work. When the wrapped stitch is reached on the subsequent row, work the wrap loop and the wrapped stitch together, to close the gap between the wrapped stitch and the adjacent stitch.

Finishing a shawl

One of the great characteristics of knitted fabric is that is can be gently manipulated, steamed or blocked into a final shape. The shape does not need to be the exact original shape knitted. Known as finishing, dressing or blocking, this final step is where the shawl is set to the desired shape and measurements. By adding these finishing touches, curves can be added to straight lines, points can be extended, and a stitch pattern can be revealed. For example, a shawl can begin with a single point, with increases being worked on one side to make a triangle. This shawl can then continue as a rectangle, before being completed with a matching triangle, where the knitting is decreased on one side. When drawn out as a shape, this shawl has sharp points and straight lines. However, once the shawl is pinned out on the blocking mat, the straight lines can be gently eased into a curve; in this way, straight edges of two triangles and a rectangle can be made into a curved outer edge.

Although it is tempting to miss out these finishing steps, a shawl can only really become a shawl after it has been blocked and dressed. During these final steps, the stitches relax, the pattern is opened out, and the edgings become more defined.

A shawl can be wet blocked, by gently submerging it in water, or steam blocked, by carefully using steam from an iron. Try your preferred blocking method on a small swatch of yarn before applying the method

The Cardiff Bay Shawl lower-edge centre section, showing the short-row-shaping extended edging.

to the final shawl. Different yarns and fibres behave differently when wet or with steam applied, and it is always worth testing to see which method gives you the most preferred result, and this also avoids unfortunate surprises.

If using the wet-blocking method, a product such as Soak can be added to the water. There is no need to rinse. This type of product can help to relax the yarn fibres and create a uniform finish across the whole of the knitted fabric. After submerging the shawl until it is fully wet, carefully pick it up and then wrap it in a clean towel. Gently press out as much excess water as possible. The next step is to pin out the shawl to shape on a stable surface. This could be a blocking mat, foam interlocking mats, a carpet covered with a towel or sheet or even a spare-bed mattress. The most important factor is to be able to leave the pinned-out shawl to dry completely before unpinning.

For steam blocking, the same undisturbed area is required. Pin the shawl to the measurements and shape required, then hover a steam iron over the whole area of the shawl. Be sure that the surface below the steam is heat-tolerant.

CHAPTER 3

EDGINGS AND BORDERS

Edgings and borders can refer to a cast-on, a cast-off, a shawl side or a surrounding pattern for a shawl. An edging essentially frames the shawl. In the same way that framing a picture can have a profound effect on the picture itself, the choice of shawl edging or border is critical to the overall design.

From a straightforward garter-stitch edging of only a few stitches to an elaborate lace design, the edging stitch pattern can enhance or detract from the main-shawl pattern. A shawl shape knitted in garter stitch could be surrounded and enhanced by a complex lace edging. Conversely, a garter-stitch edging can provide structure and stability for a complex openwork design. However, if an edging pattern is too complex, it can overwhelm the design; conversely, if it is too simple, the shawl shape and structure may not be held in place properly.

The same edging pattern can be used around the whole shawl, or each edge of the shawl could have a different pattern. The choice depends on the shape of the shawl and the chosen stitch patterns. Depending on the complexity of the design, there may be several suitable edging patterns. For example, a right-angled triangular shawl will have a straight edge, an increase edge and a cast-off edge. A decision about which edging to use is required for each of these options. Including one or more of the edgings as part of the overall shawl stitch pattern is a very useful way to create a unified design, without the additional step of adding the edging after the knitting of the shawl body.

In many traditional shawl designs, the edgings or borders are worked in a particular order. These construction techniques are part of a long heritage of creating certain shawl styles that have evolved to mini-mize seams and interruptions to the shawl patterning. In some cases, the decorative border is worked first, before the shawl body. Having a separate border section allows for enhanced, complex, decorative patterning. Borders can also be grafted or sewn into place after the knitting of the shawl body. The construction order can sometimes be very challenging, but it can also provide an extremely enjoyable element to the shawl-knitting experience.

For the shawl patterns included within this book, the choice of edging has been considered at the same time as designing the main pattern. All of the shawl patterns relate to the original inspirational source selected. For example, the stepped edging of the Modernism Shawl (see Chapter 11) was inspired by an outdoor staircase of a desert-modern-style building in Palm Springs, California, USA.

This chapter will demonstrate how to develop edging patterns from sources that can be worked alongside many different shawl shapes. The examples show how an edging can be developed and adapted in stages. As the inspiration is the key to the whole design, it is recommended to compile your own gallery of edging-pattern inspirations. Collect images that have personal meaning as and when you come across them. Have these available and ready to go when designing main-shawl patterns.

A single inspirational source can lead to many differ-ent versions of edging designs and customized stitch patterns. When working from inspirational sources, the aim is to capture the essence of a pattern in a way that can be applied to different edgings, rather than decide on one pattern that can be used only in a certain direction on a particular edge. By using inspiration this way, it is possible to expand your own personal stitch-pattern library in many different ways. This creates a large number of options to customize shawl patterns to suit your own style and interests.

Designing Edgings and Borders

This section explores designing a variety of different edgings from an inspirational source. These designs can be used as a stitch-pattern library or directory, as a basis for further customization, or as a starting point for completely new designs. The design stages can be applied to your own inspirational sources, to assist you in creating new customized edging patterns.

The inspirational source for this section is located in the Agora, a public plaza in the heart of the European Parliament in Brussels, Belgium. Here, there are several fascinating buildings with interesting architectural features and decorative details and, therefore, many inspirational possibilities for shawl-edging designs. The first step is to consider the inspirational source to determine what catches your attention. For this example, my focus was a small repeating pattern detail running the whole way up the side of a building. My photograph and sketch show the main elements of the design that will be represented in knitting.

Lengthwise edgings

The edging patterns of this group are worked over multiples of rows, with the same number of stitches being maintained throughout. Lengthwise edgings

The Agora public plaza, European Parliament, Brussels, Belgium.

Decorative detail of a building in the Agora public plaza, European Parliament, Brussels, Belgium.

Information Common to All Edging Swatches in This Section

Inspiration: Architectural detail, Agora public plaza, Brussels, Belgium
Test yarn shown: Rowan Baby Merino Silk DK (66-per-cent wool, 34-per-cent silk, 135m/147yd per 50g ball).
Shade Dawn; 1 × 50g skein, approximately 10g required for each swatch
Needles: A pair 4mm (UK 8/US 6) knitting needles, unless otherwise stated

Special Abbreviations

kfb: knit front and back – knit into the front and then the back of the next stitch on the left-hand needle, then allow this knitted-into stitch to slip off of the left-hand needle point (1st inc'd)
mb: make bobble – (k1, yo) twice, k1 all into the next stitch, turn and p5, turn and k5, turn and p2tog, p1, p2tog, turn and sl1, k2tog, psso

can be knitted vertically along the sides of a straight-edged shawl body. Alternatively, a lengthwise edging can be knitted on to the live stitches of an outer edge of a shawl, as is possible, for example, for a circular shawl. One stitch of the edging is worked together with one live stitch at the end of every right-side row, resulting in gradual casting off of the live stitches and formation of a decorative, stretchy border pattern.

The patterns explored in this section represent the architectural detail by using combinations of garter-stitch ridges and bobbles. The outer edge of the pattern includes a slipped stitch. This helps to hold the stitches in place neatly. There is also a three-stitch garter-stitch ridge at this outer edge, again to keep the edging neat. However, a consequence of the slip-stitch and garter-stitch combination can be a tight edge. Swatching will reveal whether this is a problem. The inner edge of the stitch pattern is closest to the main-shawl pattern. It can be adjusted in width, or removed completely, to suit the main-shawl design.

A prominent textured bobble has been selected to represent the long line of circular features of the building's decorative panel. A larger or smaller bobble could be used in the same stitch position. The bobble in this swatch requires the work to be turned during the knit-

ting. An alternative bobble could be knitted over two rows (with stitches being increased on the first row and decreased on the subsequent row), which may be more pleasurable to work as a shawl increases in size.

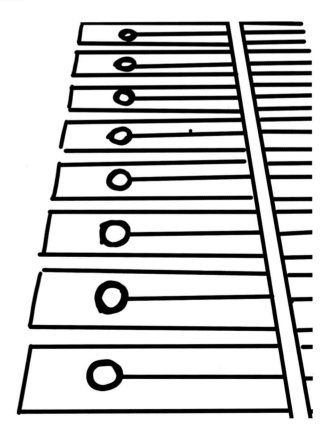

Sketch of the decorative detail of a building in the Agora public plaza, European Parliament, Brussels, Belgium.

Lengthwise Agora Edgings 1 and 2

Swatch information

Increases: None
Decreases: None
Start: Cast-on edge
Centre: Work in pattern
End: Cast-off edge
Border (inner edge): Garter stitch
Border (outer edge): Slipped stitch

Swatch instructions

Using yarn of choice and appropriate needle size, cast on 14sts.

Next, work rows 1–6 of Agora edging 1 or 2 until desired length of swatch is reached.

Cast off knitwise.

Block swatch according to instructions on yarn ball band.

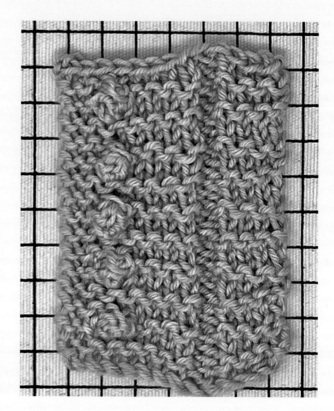

RIGHT: Swatch of Agora edging 1, with five repeats of rows 1–6.

BELOW: Charts of Agora edgings 1 and 2.

Stitch patterns

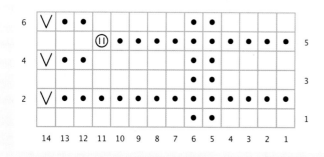

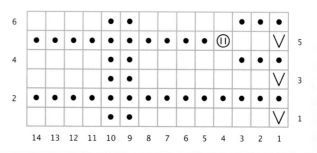

	RS: knit WS: purl	●	RS: purl WS: knit	ⓘⓘ	mb	V	slip

Agora edging 1, worked over 14sts and 6 rows

Row 1 (RS): K4, p2, k8.
Row 2 (WS): Sl1 wyif, k13.
Row 3: As row 1.
Row 4: Sl1 wyif, k2, p5, k2, p4.
Row 5: P10, mb, k3.
Row 6: As row 4.

Agora edging 2, worked over 14sts and 6 rows

Row 1 (RS): Sl1, k7, p2, k4.
Row 2 (WS): Knit.
Row 3: As row 1.
Row 4: P4, k2, p5, k3.
Row 5: Sl1, k2, mb, p10.
Row 6: As row 4.

Yarn and swatching

The test yarn selected for the following swatches is Rowan Baby Merino Silk DK. This wool-and-silk double-knit (DK)-weight yarn provides a combination of excellent stitch definition and a slight silky sheen. The stitch definition is important for the appearance of the reverse-stocking-stitch ridges. The silky sheen represents the metallic architectural feature of the inspiration.

The patterns Agora edging 1 and 2 are worked over fourteen stitches and multiples of six rows. These edgings are worked lengthwise. Charts are provided for both mirror-imaged edgings, allowing matching edgings to be worked on two opposite sides of a shawl, if desired. The knitted swatch shown is for Agora edging 1. There are five repeats of the six-row pattern in the sample swatch.

Developing the lengthwise edging designs

Once the initial pattern versions have been designed, subsequent developments can extend the pattern, while continuing to keep the essence of the design. Through this process, the stitch pattern can be altered to suit the shawl design and to create different frames or borders. The first step is to extend the initial sketch, exploring ways that the lines, shapes and details of the inspiration can be applied.

The angle at which the inspirational photograph was taken can suggest a change in the width of the pattern. In the image, the pattern appears wider at the lower edge and narrower at the top. This implies a knitted edging that changes in width. Ways to achieve this result include adding or removing stitches at the beginning or end of the rows or between the bobble and the beginning or end of the row. This will alter the width of the edging, making it narrower or wider, depending on the requirements of the shawl design.

To illustrate this case, four different ideas have been considered. These ideas include shaping the outer edge of the border in different ways; removing some of the garter-stitch detail, to create more open space around the bobbles; and considering the horizontal

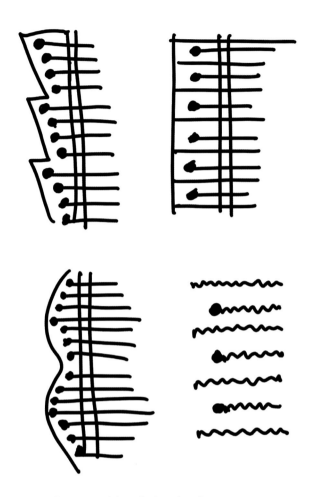

Sketches of Agora-edging design developments.

lines only, without the vertical detail. Each option will be considered in this section.

In the patterns for Agora edgings 3 and 4, the stitch pattern has been extended to create a curved edge. Stitches are increased at the outer edges to widen the knitting. After the widest point is reached, the stitches are decreased until the same number of stitches as that cast on at the beginning is reached. The outer edge has also been altered in this sample, with two garter-stitch ridges being removed. This creates more space around the bobble, making it a more prominent feature. Agora edgings 3 and 4 are worked over eleven to fourteen stitches and multiples of forty-two rows. This edging is worked lengthwise. Charts are provided for both mirror-imaged edgings. The knitted swatch shown is for Agora edging 3.

Lengthwise Agora Edgings 3 and 4

Swatch information

Increase: Kfb
Decreases: K2tog, ssk
Start: Cast-on edge
Centre: Work in pattern
End: Cast-off edge
Border (inner edge): Garter stitch
Border (outer edge): Slipped stitch

Swatch instructions

Using yarn of choice and appropriate needle size, cast on 11sts.

Next, work rows 1–42 of Agora edging 3 or 4 until desired length of swatch is reached.

Cast off knitwise.

Block swatch according to instructions on yarn ball band.

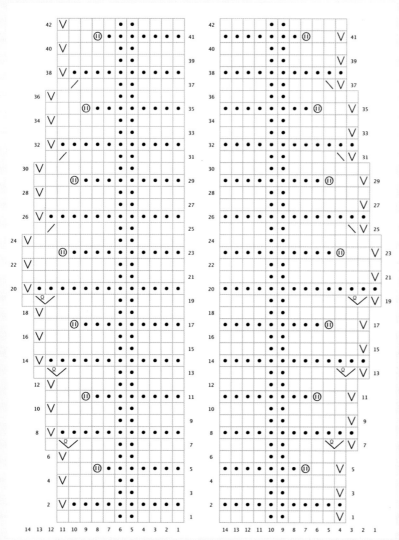

Charts of Agora edgings 3 and 4.

Stitch patterns

Agora edging 3, worked over 11 base stitches and 42 rows

Row 1 (RS): K4, p2, k5.
Row 2 (WS): Sl1 wyif, k10.
Row 3: As row 1.
Row 4: Sl1 wyif, p4, k2, p4.
Row 5: P7, mb, k3.
Row 6: As row 4.
Row 7: K4, p2, k3, kfb, k1. (12sts, with 1st inc'd)
Row 8: Sl1 wyif, k11.
Row 9: K4, p2, k6.
Row 10: Sl1 wyif, p5, k2, p4.
Row 11: P8, mb, k3.
Row 12: As row 10.
Row 13: K4, p2, k4, kfb, k1. (13sts, with 1st inc'd)
Row 14: Sl1 wyif, k12.
Row 15: K4, p2, k7.
Row 16: Sl1 wyif, p6, k2, p4.
Row 17: P9, mb, k3.
Row 18: As row 16.
Row 19: K4, p2, k5, kfb, k1. (14sts, with 1st inc'd)
Row 20: Sl1 wyif, k13.
Row 21: K4, p2, k8.
Row 22: Sl1 wyif, p7, k2, p4.
Row 23: P10, mb, k3.

Key

☐	RS: knit / WS: purl
•	RS: purl / WS: knit
⑪	mb
V	slip
Ⓥ	RS: knit into fb / WS: purl into fb
/	RS: k2tog / WS: p2tog
\	RS: ssk / WS: ssp

Row 37: K4, p2, k3, k2tog, k1. (11sts, with 1st dec'd)
Row 38: As row 2.
Row 39: As row 1.
Rows 40–41: As rows 4–5.
Row 42: As row 4.

Agora edging 4, worked over 11 base stitches and 42 rows

Row 1 (RS): Sl1, k4, p2, k4.
Row 2 (WS): Knit.
Row 3: As row 1.
Row 4: P4, k2, p5.
Row 5: Sl1, k2, mb, p7.
Row 6: As row 4.
Row 7: Sl1, kfb, k3, p2, k4. (12sts, with 1st inc'd)
Row 8: As row 2.
Row 9: Sl1, k5, p2, k4.
Row 10: P4, k2, p6.
Row 11: Sl1, k2, mb, p8.
Row 12: As row 10.
Row 13: Sl1, kfb, k4, p2, k4. (13sts, with 1st inc'd)
Row 14: As row 2.
Row 15: Sl1, k6, p2, k4.
Row 16: P4, k2, p7.
Row 17: Sl1, k2, mb, p9.
Row 18: As row 16.
Row 19: Sl1, kfb, k5, p2, k4. (14sts, with 1st inc'd)
Row 20: As row 2.
Row 21: Sl1, k7, p2, k4.
Row 22: P4, k2, p8.
Row 23: Sl1, k2, mb, p10.
Row 24: As row 22.
Row 25: Sl1, ssk, k5, p2, k4. (13sts, with 1st dec'd)
Rows 26–29: As rows 14–17.
Row 30: As row 16.
Row 31: Sl1, ssk, k4, p2, k4. (12sts, with 1st dec'd)
Rows 32–35: As rows 8–11.
Row 36: As row 10.
Row 37: Sl1, ssk, k3, p2, k4. (11sts, with 1st dec'd)
Row 38: As row 2.
Row 39: As row 1.
Rows 40–41: As rows 4–5.
Row 42: As row 4.

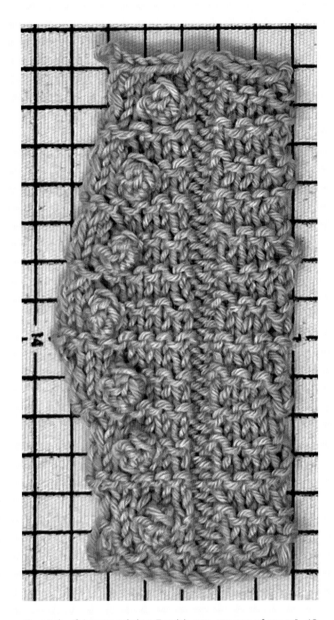

Swatch of Agora edging 3, with one repeat of rows 1–42.

Row 24: As row 22.
Row 25: K4, p2, k5, k2tog, k1. (13sts, with 1st dec'd)
Rows 26–29: As rows 14–17.
Row 30: As row 16.
Row 31: K4, p2, k4, k2tog, k1. (12sts, with 1st dec'd)
Rows 32–35: As rows 8–11.
Row 36: As row 10.

Lengthwise Agora Edgings 5 and 6

Swatch instructions

Using yarn of choice and appropriate needle size, cast on 11sts.

Rows 1–23: Work as rows 1–23 of Agora edging 3 or 4.

Row 24: Cast off 3sts, patt to end.

The previous 24 rows set the edging pattern.

Rep these 24 rows once more or until desired length of swatch is reached.

Cast off knitwise.

Block swatch according to instructions on yarn ball band.

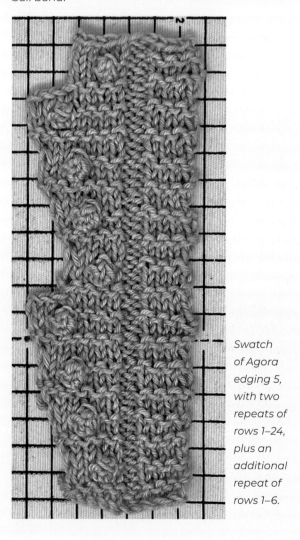

Swatch of Agora edging 5, with two repeats of rows 1–24, plus an additional repeat of rows 1–6.

Widthwise Agora Edgings 7 and 8

Swatch instructions

Note: Each stitch pattern is a multiple of 8sts plus an additional 7 stitches. The stitches of the stitch multiples are shown within the coloured boxes of the charted pattern and referred to within the asterisked instructions of the written pattern.

Using yarn of choice and appropriate needle size, cast on 23sts.

Row 1 (RS): Work stitches 1–8 of Agora edging 7 or 8 twice, then complete the row by working stitches 9–15 of the selected stitch pattern.

Row 2 (WS): Work stitches 15–9 of the selected stitch pattern once, then complete the row by working stitches 8–1 of the selected stitch pattern twice.

The previous 2 rows set the edging pattern.

Continue as set by the previous 2 rows, working following row of stitch pattern for each subsequent row of edging as required, until Agora edging 7 or 8 row 6 has been completed.

Next, work these 2 rows twice more, or until desired length of swatch is achieved.

Cast off knitwise.

Block swatch according to instructions on yarn ball band.

Stitch patterns

Agora edging 7 (cast-on border), worked over a multiple of 8sts, plus 7sts, and 6 rows

Row 1 (RS): *P3, mb, p3, k1; rep from * twice, p3, mb, p3.

Row 2 (WS): K3, p1, k3, *(p1, k3) × 2; rep from * twice.

Row 3: *(P3, k1) × 2; rep from * twice, p3, k1, p3.

Row 4: As row 2.

Rows 5–6: Knit.

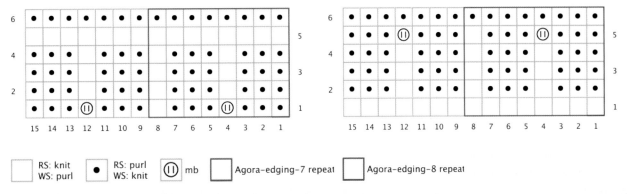

☐ RS: knit WS: purl	• RS: purl WS: knit	⒒ mb	☐ Agora-edging-7 repeat	☐ Agora-edging-8 repeat

Charts of Agora edgings 7 and 8.

Agora edging 8 (cast-off border), worked over a multiple of 8sts, plus 7sts, and 6 rows

Row 1 (RS): Knit.

Row 2 (WS): K3, p1, k3, *(p1, k3) × 2; rep from * twice.

Row 3: *(P3, k1) × 2; rep from * twice, p3, k1, p3.

Row 4: As row 2.

Row 5: *P3, mb, p3, k1; rep from * twice, p3, mb, p3.

Row 6: Knit.

Swatches of Agora edging 7 (cast-on edging; lower swatch) and 8 (cast-off edging; upper swatch).

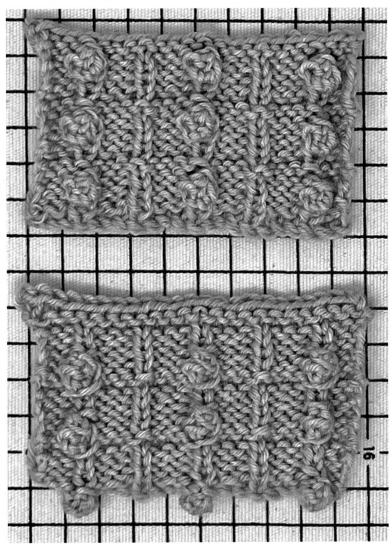

Agora edgings 5 and 6 are created by using a section of the patterns and charts for Agora edgings 3 and 4: first, rows one to twenty-three of Agora edging 3 or 4 are worked; second, on the twenty-fourth row, three stitches are cast off at the beginning of the row. By casting off a small number of stitches every twenty-four rows, an asymmetric zigzag edge is created.

To summarize, Agora edgings 5 and 6 are worked over eleven to fourteen stitches and multiples of twenty-four rows. This edging is worked lengthwise. Refer to the written instructions or charts for Agora edgings 3 and 4, rows 1–24. The knitted swatch shown is for Agora edging 5.

Stitch-multiple (widthwise) edgings

The previous edging patterns have all been worked lengthwise. Designing patterns to be repeated across multiples of stitches follows the same process as for designing the lengthwise patterns. For the widthwise Agora edgings, the aim is to reflect the essence of the design in the combination of straight lines and bobbles. The lines are represented by a single line of vertical knit stitches on a reverse-stocking-stitch background. Bobbles are placed on the vertical lines of knit stitches. These stitch patterns are a related design that is worked in a different direction to the previous lengthwise edgings. The vertical lines provide contrast to the horizontal ridged lines of Agora edgings 1–6.

These edgings are worked over multiples of stitches and can be made as wide as required by the pattern. The knitted swatches for Agora edgings 7 and 8 are worked over twenty-three stitches. These patterns have two eight-stitch repeats plus an additional seven stitches. These swatches have been worked with 3.25mm needles, as knitting with a smaller needle size creates a firm, stable edge.

Edging Placement

There are several ways to add edgings to a shawl design. Edgings can be worked at the same time as the main-shawl pattern. They can also be added afterwards, being sewn in place, stitches being picked up and worked outwards, or being grafted on to live stitches. This allows stitch patterns to be worked in multiple directions.

Each shawl shape will have its own requirements for placing edgings. These will be considered in examples throughout this book. In this section, the edge-to-edge rectangle shape is used to illustrate some of the options available. The two accompanying diagrams show two options for considering the edgings of a rectangular shawl that is knitted lengthwise. The edgings can be knitted along with the central rectangle or added afterwards, if appropriate. For the following examples, only integral edgings, that is, those knitted as part of the shawl body, are considered.

These diagrams can be very helpful as, with measurements placed on to the dimension lines, they will also allow the addition of figures for stitches and rows. In many patterns, versions of these diagrams are known as schematics. Once the measurements are added, the diagrams can be used as a guide for blocking the completed shawl.

The edge-to-edge rectangles begin with a cast-on pattern, usually worked with a smaller needle size. Construction then proceeds with the main-shawl pattern, with side edgings being worked at the same time. The shawl is completed with a cast-off edge.

In option 1, the cast-on and cast-off edges extend across the whole width of the shawl. The side edges are worked between them as part of the main pattern. In option 2, the side edges can extend from the cast-on edge to the cast-off edge. The cast-on and cast-off edges are worked between the side edges.

The decision on which option to use will be guided by the inspirational source and the style to be achieved. Option 1 is first sketched out here, with the cast-on and cast-off edges extending across the full width of the rectangle. Extending the side edges for the full length of the shape, as next sketched out for option 2, emphasizes the appearance of the length of the design. Sketching ideas in this way can really help with making these decisions. A quick drawing of the proposed layout is an excellent way to see how the different patterns work together.

There are no 'right' or 'wrong' answers to these deci-

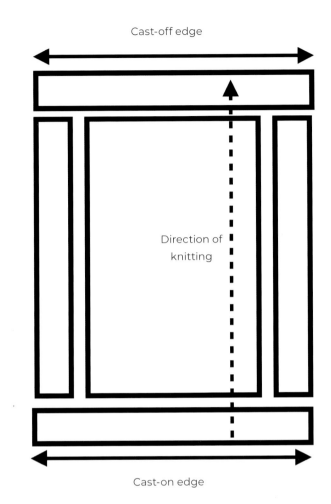

Cast-off edge

Direction of knitting

Cast-on edge

Rectangle with edgings: option 1.

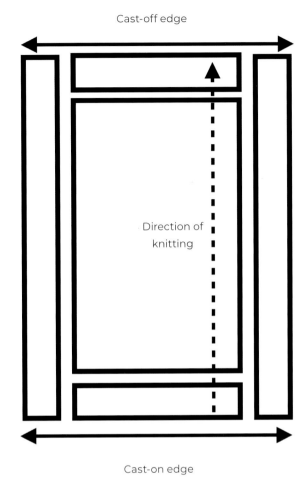

Cast-off edge

Direction of knitting

Cast-on edge

Rectangle with edgings: option 2.

sions. The chosen way forward should always reflect the design intention. In this case, the original source image and drawing were of an architectural feature that was located on the side of a building. This series of small patterned sections gave the impression of great length. For this reason, the most appropriate design version would be where the side edging begins at the cast-on edge, elongating the long edges of the shawl.

Knitting a multi-edging test swatch

Having made the main design decisions, the patterns are then all tested together in a swatch. For a full-size shawl, separate tension swatches are also knitted for the main stitch patterns. From these additional tension swatches, the number of stitches and rows for the actual shawl dimensions can be calculated.

For this test-swatch example, the main pattern is an extension of the edging pattern and consists of garter-stitch ridges on a stocking-stitch background. This stitch pattern is worked over a multiple of one stitch and six rows. This means that any number of stitches can be included in the pattern. However, groups of six rows must be worked to achieve the ridge pattern.

- The side edging is worked over eight stitches and six rows.

- The cast-on edging is worked over a multiple of eight stitches plus an additional seven stitches, to balance the pattern, and six rows.
- The cast-off edging is worked over a multiple of eight stitches plus seven stitches and six rows.

The total number of cast-on edge stitches is calculated by adding together the cast-on edge-pattern stitches plus the stitches of the left and right edging patterns. For the sample swatch, the centre pattern is one repeat of the cast-on edging, plus the extra stitches required

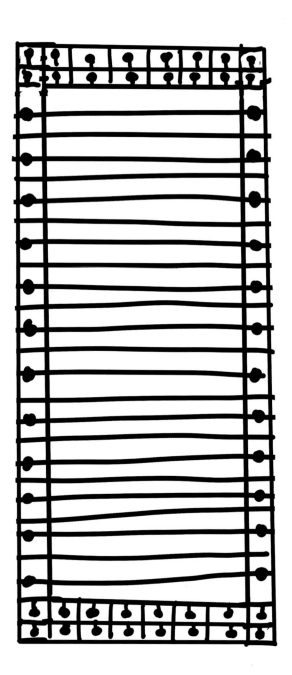

Sketch of edge-to-edge rectangle with full-width cast-on and cast-off edgings (option 1).

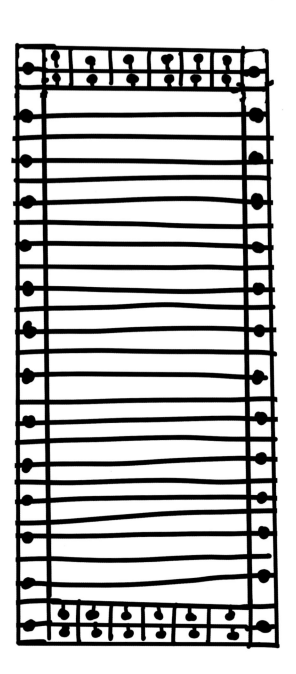

Sketch of edge-to-edge rectangle with full-length side edgings (option 2).

Agora-Pattern Multi-Edging

Swatch instructions
Using yarn of choice and a smaller needle size than to be used for working the main-pattern part of the swatch, cast on 31sts.

Lower edging
Row 1 (RS): Work as Agora-Pattern row 1.
Row 2 (WS): Work as Agora-Pattern row 2.
Rows 3–6: Work as Agora-Pattern rows 3–6.
The previous 6 rows set the lower-edging pattern.
Work these 6 rows once more, using Agora-Pattern rows 1–6 as set.

Change to using the main (larger) needles for working the main-pattern part of the swatch.

Main pattern
Row 1 (RS): Work as Agora-Pattern row 7.

Row 2 (WS): Work as Agora-Pattern row 8.
Rows 3–6: Work as Agora-Pattern rows 9–12.
The previous 6 rows set the main pattern.
Work these 6 rows another two times, using Agora-Pattern rows 7–12 as set.

Change to using the smaller needles.

Upper edging
Row 1 (RS): Work as Agora-Pattern row 13.
Row 2 (WS): Work as Agora-Pattern row 14.
Rows 3–6: Work as Agora-Pattern rows 15–18.
The previous 6 rows set the upper-edging pattern.
Work rows 1–5 once more, using Agora-Pattern rows 13–17 as set.
Next, with WS facing, cast off in patt.
Block swatch according to instructions on yarn ball band.

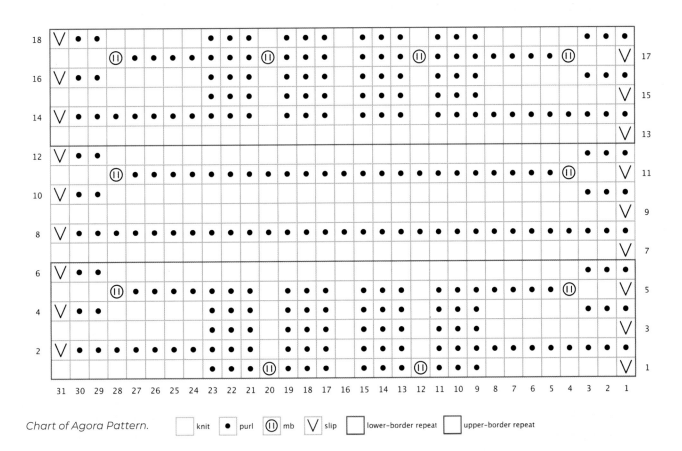

Chart of Agora Pattern. ☐ knit • purl ⓘ mb V slip ☐ lower-border repeat ☐ upper-border repeat

Stitch pattern

Agora Pattern, worked over 31sts and multiples of 6 rows

Row 1 (RS): Sl1, k7, p3, mb, p3, k1, p3, mb, p3, k8.

Row 2 (WS): Sl1 wyif, k10, (p1, k3) × 2, p1, k11.

Row 3: Sl1, k7, (p3, k1) × 3, p3, k8.

Row 4: Sl1 wyif, k2, p5, (k3, p1) × 3, k3, p5, k3.

Row 5: Sl1, k2, mb, p7, (k1, p3) × 2, k1, p7, mb, k3.

Row 6: Sl1 wyif, k2, p25, k3.

Row 7: Sl1, k30.

Row 8: Sl1 wyif, k30.

Row 9: As row 7.

Row 10: As row 6.

Row 11: Sl1, k2, mb, p23, mb, k3.

Row 12: As row 6.

Row 13: As row 7.

Rows 14–16: As rows 2–4.

Row 17: Sl1, k2, mb, p7, mb, p3, k1, p3, mb, p7, mb, k3.

Row 18: As row 4.

Agora-Pattern multi-edging test swatch.

to make a balanced repeat. This totals fifteen stitches. The side edgings comprise eight stitches each. The number of stitches needed for the sample cast-on is therefore thirty-one stitches.

For the number of rows, one repeat of the side edging is six rows. One repeat of the cast-on edging can be worked over these rows. To extend the pattern, two repeats of the rows are worked. This can be mirror-imaged for the cast-off edging, with all stitches being cast off together on the final pattern row. There are a total of sixteen rows to be worked at each end of the sample. For the main section of the sample swatch, three pattern repeats of six rows are worked.

The swatch pattern will have the same basic structure as a full shawl pattern. Writing out these instructions as a pattern has the benefit of keeping track of what has been knitted and tested. This can be used for future reference. Creating a chart, using graph paper or charting software, is another way to record a summary of the swatch pattern and is extremely useful for reference throughout the design process.

Elements of the previous edging patterns have been used for this swatch pattern. However, some adjustments and refinements have been made. This demonstrates that the design process is continually changing and evolving. Until the final pattern is confirmed, refinements can always continue to be made!

Analysing a multi-edging test swatch

It is always important to look closely at a test swatch. Decide what went well and what did not work. Look for any improvements that can be made. This may mean working another swatch, but this is definitely worthwhile. Try not to undo swatches while working on developments. It can be hard to remember exactly what went right and wrong, without such a tangible visual reminder.

For this rectangular test swatch, there are a couple of key points to note:

- The effect on the bobbles of changing the needle size is very clear. Bobbles knitted with the larger size of needles are much larger and more prominent than those knitted with the smaller needles.
- The contrast between horizontal and vertical lines shows up really well. The edgings are made more interesting by involving several different, yet related, stitch patterns.

A further development to be considered includes having the vertical lines of the edge pattern across the whole of the cast-on and cast-off borders. Although this would have a visual effect on the long side borders, the pattern could work very well. It is also well worth experimenting with using more than one shade of yarn. Working every ridge, or selected ridges, in a contrasting yarn shade would add another dimension to the design.

Edging Patterns and Shawl Shapes

When working with other shawl shapes, such as triangles, circles and crescents, the same principles apply. Begin with the inspiration for the whole design. This inspiration may be sourced from your own library of images and sketches, collected over a period of time, or from an image or sketch in this book. Whichever shape of shawl you are working with, sketch out the design and look for the important interactions of the different shawl sections. As examples, a circular shawl could have a single edging pattern that extents outwards from the main design; a triangular shawl may have three completely different edging patterns, each worked in a different shade or yarn. The most important factor is to create a unified design, where all of the different elements relate to each other.

Part 2
INDIVIDUAL SHAWL SHAPES

INTRODUCTION

Finding inspiration in the world around us is an excellent way to develop new and original designs for shawls; for example, ceramic tiles on a building wall can be a wonderful starting point for a square shawl. To demonstrate this design process, example source images are located alongside the designs throughout this book. The many possibilities for design development are further explored through sketches and written descriptions of the design process. When selecting your own inspirational sources, look for shapes and patterns that catch your eye and try to take a photo, make notes or draw an outline sketch, or try all of the above. By doing this, you can capture your thoughts and have your ideas ready to refer to at any time.

OPPOSITE: Circular drain cover, Schleissheim Palace and Park, Germany.

The shape of a shawl is critical to the design process. The way that shape and stitch pattern interact together determines the success of the design. It is therefore important to consider possible shapes for the shawl design right at the start of the project. Knitting small test swatches can be really helpful at this stage, allowing ideas to be generated and tested.

Part 2 of this book concentrates on providing practical advice, giving step-by-step instructions on how to knit a range of small, individual shawl shapes. These individual shapes are like building blocks and can be used separately or together to create a range of new composite shape shawls. These are looked at in later chapters. Part 2 includes instructions for knitting small samples of straight-sided shapes, such as squares, rectangles and triangles, followed by curved shapes, including circles, semicircles and crescents.

Along with inspirational source images, the examples in this section are accompanied by an image of a knitted swatch. Detailed pattern instructions describe how to knit a similar swatch in the yarn of your choice.

These small swatches can be used as a blank canvas, where stitch patterns and shaping techniques can be customized and tested. Small test swatches are also an excellent way to sample a variety of yarns, to assess whether the final effect is the one that you wish to achieve.

The swatches are all knitted with stocking stitch and a garter-stitch border. Using the same stitch pattern throughout the sections allows a comparison between different shapes to be made. Additionally, techniques for increasing and decreasing are clearly visible within the chosen basic stitch pattern. A garter-stitch border is used to provide stability to the swatch and prevents the edges from curling. Each swatch has been blocked, again to clearly show the techniques being demonstrated.

Typically, a contrasting stripe is worked approximately halfway through each shape, to demonstrate the effect of horizontal pattern placement. Pattern placement within a shape can be horizontal, vertical, diagonal or radial, or combinations of all of these. More complex pattern placement and combinations, such as asymmetrical and mirror-imaged patterns, will be considered in the shawl-project chapters.

It is possible to extend the swatches to make larger shapes, either for use as tension swatches or even to become a full-size shawl. Tension swatches should be large enough for at least a ten-centimetre-square measurement to be taken for both stitches and rows.

Designing With Shapes

A shawl can comprise only a single shape or it can be made up of multiple smaller shapes. Within these shape combinations, the placement of pattern will alter depending on the orientation of the shape or shapes. Pattern can therefore potentially be added in different directions. This is one reason that it is so important to break down a shawl design into component parts before building it back up again to create a unified design. Looking at each of the smaller shapes individually provides an idea of the effect that each individual design choice will have on the whole design.

A shape-based or modular approach to knitting construction can refer to using specific blocks of knitting that, when combined, create a larger defined shape. Additionally, it can also refer to larger-scale combinations of shapes that provide the framework in which to create designs on different scales and with multiple patterns and techniques. This difference in scale is very important. A shawl can comprise many small modules or several larger modules.

One of the first designers to explore a shape-based approach to shawl design was Virginia Woods Bellamy (1890–1976). Her book *Number Knitting: The New All-Ways-Stretch Method* was published in 1952. Here, Woods Bellamy sets out a series of shapes, mainly knitted in garter stitch, that can be combined to create a knitted fabric that stretches in all directions. The system is a form of modular knitting based on seven distinct shapes. Her system of modular construction resulted in accessories and garments that had beautiful drape and wonderful elasticity within the knitted fabric. Based on these seven shapes, a wide variety of complex knitting could be developed.

An article for *Piecework* in February 2020, written by A Braaten and S Strawn, describes the method:

> Virginia Woods Bellamy described number knitting as 'merely a method of knitting design based on squares and triangles and the tributary units'. She discarded the traditional measurements for geometrical principles. She began each design by selecting among seven knitted geometric units, then drew the design on graph paper unit by unit, and numbered each unit in the order in which it would be knitted.

The article goes on to describe the next steps in the process:

> Following the graph as a pattern, she knitted loosely in garter stitch on large needles, picking up stitches along edges unit by unit.

Modular-knitting techniques have been explored and developed by innovative designers such as Alison Ellen, Vivian Høxbro, Melissa Leapman and the designers together known as Woolly Thoughts. By examining modular-knitting techniques and applying them in many different ways, these creative designers have opened up many exciting possibilities for shawl and garment design.

Alison Ellen in particular explores the way that different stitch patterns interact with each other, creating exciting knitted-fabric possibilities. By changing just one aspect of a stitch pattern, the whole appearance of the knitted fabric can be modified. For example, a garter-stitch modular square looks and behaves completely differently if worked in a rib pattern over the same number of stitches and rows.

In *Knitting Modular: Shawls, Wraps, and Stoles*, published in 2018, Melissa Leapman explores the use of combined wedges of shapes to create beautiful shawl designs. Through a seven-step process, she guides her readers to create their own shawl versions. A particularly beautiful design example is her parallelogram, formed by combining triangle shapes. This is a great example where the overall shape of the shawl is a rectangle. However, the modular elements within this rectangle are triangles.

The following chapters explore shawl shapes and their design possibilities. Individual shapes are considered first, before moving on to more complex combinations of shapes. Each section shows the design development from the initial inspiration through to the individual shape and includes photos and sketches to illustrate the process.

CHAPTER 4

SQUARES

A square is a shape with four equal sides at right angles to one another. The square shape in shawl design is extremely versatile and can be used in many different ways and at different scales. A single square can be the overall shape of a whole shawl. Alternatively, it can be a small building block within one shawl section.

A square shape can also be made up of other shapes. For example, some variations of Shetland shawls are knitted with a central square surrounded by a series of rectangles with angled edges. These edges are grafted together and are in turn surrounded by another outer border. The overall shape is therefore still a square; however, it is made up of several different shapes. This type of composite shape will be considered in more detail in later sections. The focus of this chapter is on methods to make individual square shapes.

Square-shaped shawls can be worn in many different ways, folded or unfolded. A square can be folded to make a different shape, such as a triangle or a rectangle, or be partially folded so that a corner design is visible. The double layer created by folding has several effects. Folding a shawl knitted in very fine yarn can create a warm layer. If the shawl is knitted in a heavier-weight yarn then it may become very bulky. Folding also has an effect on pattern: the pattern may be obscured, or the folding may reveal a deliberate detail, depending on the intention of the shawl design. For example, a fine, woven turn-over shawl has two pattern sections worked at the opposite corners. The lower one is visible

at the bottom edge of the shawl and the other is visible after the top edge of the shawl is folded over. This shawl shows how deliberate pattern placement can be used to great effect.

The main inspiration for the square-shawl swatches in this chapter is a selection of stunning square-shaped wall tiles from the city of Lisbon, Portugal. One single decorated tile could be the inspiration for a whole shawl. A combination of several tiles could also inspire a different shawl. By looking closely at the image of the tiles, a great deal of inspiration can be found that can be used in many different ways. The guiding principle when deciding how to use inspiration in shawl design is to consider the effect that is intended. For example, linking several shapes together can create a dramatic

Information Common to All Swatches in This Section

Inspiration: Ceramic wall tiles, Lisbon, Portugal
Swatch shape: Square
Test yarn shown: baa ram ewe Titus 4ply (50-per-cent Wensleydale wool, 20-per-cent Bluefaced Leicester wool, 30-per-cent British alpaca, 320m/350yd per 100g hank)
Yarn A: Shade 003 (Parkin); 1 × 100g skein, approximately 10g required for swatch
Yarn B: Shade 008 (Coal); 1 × 100g skein, less than 5g required for swatch
Needles (smaller size): A pair 3.25mm (UK 10/US 3) knitting needles
Needles (larger size): A pair 3.5mm (UK 9–10/US 4) knitting needles

OPPOSITE: Square-shaped ceramic wall tiles, Lisbon, Portugal.

effect. Using the inspirational image of the wall tiles, it can be seen that the placement of non-patterned tiles in between the patterned tiles is very important to the overall wall design. If all of the tiles were decorated then the detail of the decorated tiles could be lost in the overall pattern. The non-decorated tiles also provide contrast to the decorated tiles. These aspects can be used to inspire a design that has sections of stocking stitch and sections of decorative stitch patterns. Alternatively, use of the different square patterns will result in a balanced shawl design.

Square Worked Edge to Edge

This edge-to-edge square is knitted by casting on a defined number of stitches, working in rows until the sides measure the same as the width of the cast-on edge, and then casting off. All four sides will be of the same measurement. The number of stitches to be cast on will be determined by the desired width measurement.

The advantage of this shape is that it is straightforward to calculate the relevant numbers for and to measure. Once the desired width of an edge has been determined, the number of stitches and rows can be calculated from a tension swatch. An edge-to-edge square can be knitted using only knit and purl stitches, with no increasing or decreasing. Edgings can be knitted at the same time as the shape or be added as a border after the knitting of the square is complete.

Horizontal stripes of pattern or colour knitted within this construction will have the appearance of straight lines. These lines can remain horizontal or become vertical or diagonal, depending on the angle of wear of the shawl. Stitch patterns can be added on predetermined rows, using a wide variety of techniques. These may affect the tension and therefore the number of rows to be worked. In this example, the square shape has a horizontal line of pattern that runs from outer edge to outer edge. This line can be placed at any location on the square, dividing the shape in different ways. For example, if the line of pattern is knitted halfway through the square, the shape is divided in half.

Square Worked Edge to Edge

Swatch information
Increases: None
Decreases: None
Start: Cast-on edge
Centre: Work in pattern
End: Cast-off edge
Border (bottom, top and side edges): Garter stitch

Swatch instructions
Note: Throughout the swatch, the first stitch of every row is slipped, to create a neat selvedge.

Lower border

Using the smaller needles and Yarn A, cast on 19sts.
Knit 4 rows, slipping the first stitch of every row.
Change to using the larger needles.

Lower swatch section

Row 1 and every following RS row: Using Yarn A, sl1, k to end.
Row 2 and every following WS row: Using Yarn A, sl1, k1, p to last 2sts, k2.
The previous 2 rows set the lower-swatch-section pattern.
Next, work these 2 rows another four times.

By placing the pattern towards the top or bottom of the square, the shape can be divided into thirds, with one-third below and two-thirds above the line, or vice versa.

The shape can be folded along horizontal, vertical or diagonal lines, forming new shapes such as a rectangle or a triangle. The weight of yarn used for the shawl can place constraints on the folding possibilities. For example, a square knitted in a lace-weight yarn will have multiple folding options, as the knitted fabric will fold and drape well, even at double

Edge-to-edge-square swatch, knitted with 3.25mm and 3.5mm needles and baa ram ewe Titus 4ply yarn.

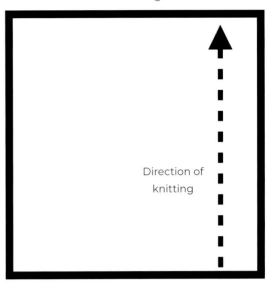

Cast-off edge

Direction of knitting

Cast-on edge

Diagram of a square worked edge to edge.

Contrast stripe

Row 1 (RS): Using Yarn B, sl1, k to end.
Row 2 (WS): Using Yarn B, sl1, k to end.

Upper swatch section

Rows 1–10: Using Yarn A, work as lower-swatch-section rows 1–2.

Upper border

Change to using the smaller needles.
Using Yarn A, knit 4 rows, slipping the first stitch of every row. Cast off knitwise.

To extend this swatch into a larger square shape, cast on additional stitches and then work additional rows until the length of the swatch sides matches the width of the cast-on edge.

thickness. However, if a heavier-weight yarn is used, folding the shawl could create too much bulk in places and therefore may be less comfortable to wear.

Square Worked Point to Point

This method of creating a square begins with a single stitch. Stitches are then increased at each end of every right-side row until the desired width (that is, the distance from the left-hand side point to the right-hand side point) of the square is reached. After this, stitches are then decreased at each end of every right-side row until a single stitch remains. All four sides of this square shape will be of the same length. Increases can be made as m1r and m1l paired increases. Decreases can be made as ssk and k2tog paired decreases.

The advantage of working this way is that the diagonal point-to-point width of the square can be decided as the stitches are increased. If a limited amount of

Square Worked Point to Point

Swatch information

Increases: M1l, m1r

Decreases: K2tog, ssk

Start: Lower point of square

Centre: Increase from point to full width then decrease to point

End: Upper point of square

Border (side edges): Garter stitch

Swatch instructions

Lower point

Using the smaller or larger needles, as preferred, and Yarn A, cast on 1st.

Row 1 (RS): Using Yarn A, k1, p1, k1 all into same st. (3sts, with 2sts inc'd)

Row 2 (WS): Using Yarn A, knit.

Row 3: Using Yarn A, k1, m1r, k to last st, m1l, k1. (5sts, with 2sts inc'd)

Row 4: Using Yarn A, knit.

Increase pattern

Row 1 (RS): Using Yarn A, k1, m1r, k to last st, m1l, k1. (7sts, with 2sts inc'd)

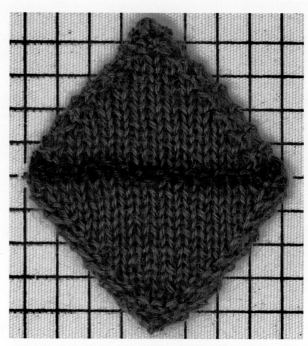

Point-to-point-square swatch, knitted with 3.5mm needles and baa ram ewe Titus 4ply yarn.

Row 2 and every following WS row: Using Yarn A, k2, p to last 2sts, k2.

yarn is available, this method allows the knitter to increase until slightly less than half of the yarn is used and then to decrease after this point of the shape knitting is reached. Although there may be a tiny amount of yarn remaining, working until slightly less than half of the yarn remains ensures that there will be enough to complete the knitting of the square.

Stitch patterns can be added on predetermined rows, using a wide variety of techniques. These may affect the tension and therefore the number of rows to be worked. Edgings can be knitted on as the shape is being formed or added as a border after the knitting is complete. Point-to-point squares require the additional knitting techniques of increasing and decreasing. The placement of any decorative stitch patterns should allow for the increases and decreases to be included in the pattern as necessary to complement the design intention.

A horizontal stitch pattern worked within this construction can have the appearance of either a diagonal or a horizontal line, depending on the angle of wear of the finished piece. As in the previous example, the pattern can be placed in the centre of the shape, creating two halves, or towards the top or bottom, to create a split of one-third to two-thirds.

Square with Single Decrease Line

This square, also known as a mitred corner, is worked with a diagonal decrease line. To knit this square, the full number of stitches required are cast on. The square is knitted in rows, with decreases worked on each side of the central stitch, usually as a double decrease. The

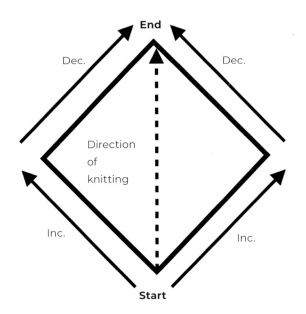

End

Dec.　　　　　　Dec.

Direction
of
knitting

Inc.　　　　　　Inc.

Start

Diagram of a square worked point to point.

The previous 2 rows set the increase pattern.
Next, work these 2 rows another six times. (19sts after final row 2 has been completed)

Contrast stripe
Row 1 (RS): Using Yarn B, knit.
Row 2 (WS): Using Yarn B, knit.

Decrease pattern
Row 1 (RS): Using Yarn A, k1, ssk, k to last 3sts, k2tog, k1. (17sts, with 2sts dec'd)
Row 2 and every following WS row: Using Yarn A, k2, p to last 2sts, k2.
The previous 2 rows set the decrease pattern.
Next, work these 2 rows another six times. (5sts after final row 2 has been completed)

Upper point
Row 1 (RS): Using Yarn A, k1, sl1, k2tog, psso, k1. (3sts, with 2sts dec'd)
Row 2 (WS): Using Yarn A, k3tog. (1st, with 2sts dec'd)
Fasten off.

To extend this swatch into a larger square shape, work additional rows with increases until the desired centre width is achieved and then work the corresponding number of rows with decreases before completing the swatch point.

diagonal decreases in this square can be worked as a decorative feature. The square is completed by decreasing to a single stitch and fastening off. The number of cast-on stitches is determined by the length of two sides of the square. Additional calculations required include allowing for accelerated decreases to be worked towards the point, to keep the square shape balanced.

Although this method of forming a square can be used for a full-size shawl, the number of stitches to cast-on would be extremely large. This type of square is commonly used as a module in a shawl made up of several similarly constructed shapes. Stitches for each additional square can be picked up from the relevant edges of the previously worked squares. This means that there is no need to sew the shapes together. By weaving ends in as you go, only blocking is required to finish the shawl.

A horizontal line of pattern knitted within this construction method will have the appearance of an 'L' or a wide 'V', depending on the shape's orientation. This line of pattern can be placed at any point on the shape to create a different balance between sections.

Square with Multiple Decrease Lines

The square with multiple decrease lines is an extension of the previous single-decrease-line example. This variation on the mitred-corner square has four decrease lines. Decreases worked at the beginning, in the middle and at the end of each flat-knitted right-side row form

Square with Single Decrease Line

Swatch information

Increases: None
Decreases: K3tog; sl1, k2tog, psso; sl1, p2tog, psso
Start: Cast-on edge of two sides of square
Centre: Decrease to upper point
End: Point of square
Border (side edges): Garter stitch
Border (cast-on edge): Garter stitch

Swatch instructions

Set-up

Using the smaller or larger needles, as preferred, and Yarn A, cast on 39sts.

Square with a single decrease line swatch, knitted with 3.5mm needles and baa ram ewe Titus 4ply yarn.

Row 1 (RS): Using Yarn A, k18, sl1, k2tog, psso, k to end. (37sts, with 2sts dec'd)
Row 2 (WS): Using Yarn A, knit.
Row 3: Using Yarn A, k17, sl1, k2tog, psso, k to end. (35sts, with 2sts dec'd)
Row 4: Using Yarn A, knit.

Lower-section decreases

Row 1: Using Yarn A, k16, sl1, k2tog, psso, k to end. (33sts, with 2sts dec'd)
Row 2: Using Yarn A, k2, p to last 2sts, k2.
The previous 2 rows set the lower-section decrease pattern, with 1st fewer being worked before and after the central decreases on every subsequent RS row. Next, work these 2 rows another four times. (25sts after final row 2 has been completed)

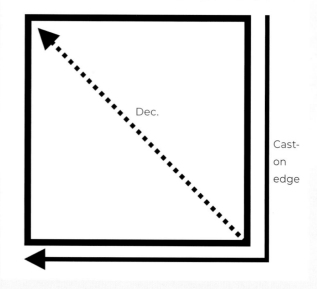

Diagram of a square with a single decrease line.

the four decrease lines when the shape is sewn up. This square begins at the cast-on edge and finishes in the centre. The square is knitted in rows, with decreases worked on every right-side row. It is completed with accelerated decreases, after which the remaining few stitches are worked together. The open side of the square is then seamed to create the completed square.

A horizontal line of pattern worked within this construction method will have the appearance of a square, with slightly elongated outer points. This effect

Contrast stripe

Row 1 (RS): Using Yarn B, work as lower-section-decreases row 1. (23sts, with 2sts dec'd)
Row 2 (WS): Using Yarn B, knit.

Upper-section decreases

Row 1 (RS): Using Yarn A, work as lower-section-decreases row 1. (21sts, with 2sts dec'd)
Row 2 (WS): Using Yarn A, p7, sl1, p2tog, psso, p to last 2sts, k2. (19sts, with 2sts dec'd)
The previous 2 rows set the upper-section decrease pattern, with 1st fewer being worked before and after the central decreases on every subsequent row.
Next, work these 2 rows another three times. (7sts after final row 2 has been completed)

Upper point

Row 1 (RS): Using Yarn A, work as lower-section-decreases row 1. (5sts, with 2sts dec'd)
Row 2 (WS): Using Yarn A, k1, sl1, k2tog, psso, k1. (3sts, with 2sts dec'd)
Row 3: Using Yarn A, k3tog.
Fasten off.

To extend this swatch into a larger square shape, cast on an odd number of stitches based on your stitch tension to correspond to the sum of the length of two sides of the square in centimetres. To ensure that decreases are worked at the centre point, subtract three stitches from the total number of cast-on stitches; divide this number by two to give the number of stitches to be worked before and after the central decreases on the first row. Next, work the alternate-row lower-section decreases at this stitch position until the majority of the square is knitted. Complete the swatch point by working the upper-section decreases on every row.

Square with Multiple Increase Lines

Instead of casting on all of the outer stitches, as in the previous example, it can be much more useful to work outwards from the centre of a square. This square is knitted by using regular increases that are in line with each corner of the square. The advantage of working this way is that the work can be continued until the desired size has been reached. At this point, there will also be live stitches available to complete the shawl with a decorative border, if desired. The border can be an extension of the main pattern, a sewn- or grafted-on separate border, or a knitted-on border. This square can be worked flat, with one seam to sew, or in the round, creating a seamless square. Horizontal patterning worked within this construction method will have the appearance of a square. Both worked-flat and in-the-round constructions begin with one or more stitches being cast on within a loop for the centre of the square; this centre-loop method is also commonly used for the centre of circles.

is a result of the decrease pattern. As with the previous example, this method of making a square has many options for including lines of pattern within the shape. Additionally, several of these squares can be used as modules and joined together to make larger shapes.

Square with Multiple Decrease Lines

Swatch information

Increases: None

Decreases: K2tog; p2tog; p2tog-tbl; p3tog; sl1, k2tog, psso; sl1, p2tog, psso; ssk

Start: Cast-on edge of four sides of square

Centre: Decrease to centre point

End: Centre of square

Border (outer edges): Garter stitch

Swatch instructions

Set-up

Using the smaller or larger needles, as preferred, and Yarn A, cast on 79sts.

Row 1 (RS): Using Yarn A, k1, k2tog, *k16, sl1, k2tog,

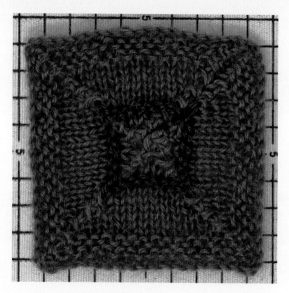

Square with multiple decrease lines swatch, knitted with 3.5mm needles and baa ram ewe Titus 4ply yarn.

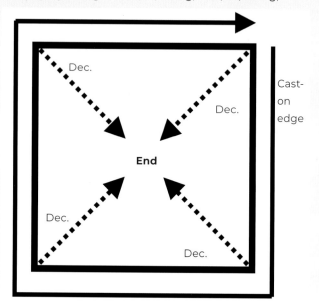

Diagram of square with multiple decrease lines.

Centre-Loop Method for a Centre Start

Step 1: Make a loop around your left forefinger, with the tail to the front and the working yarn placed over your middle finger.

Step 2: Form a yarn over with the knitting needle by inserting the needle tip under the working yarn from back to front. (1st, with 1st inc'd)

Step 3: Insert the needle tip through both yarn strands around your left forefinger and pick up the working yarn by moving the tip over and then under the working yarn.

Step 4: Pull the working yarn through both yarn strands around your left forefinger. (2sts, with 1st inc'd)

Step 1 of the centre-start centre-loop method. (Steps 1–5 photographed by Alexander Vining.)

Step 2 of the centre-start centre-loop method.

Step 3 of the centre-start centre-loop method.

psso; rep from * to last 19sts, k to last 3sts, ssk, k1. (71sts, with 8sts dec'd)

Row 2 (WS): Using Yarn A, knit.

Row 3: Using Yarn A, k1, k2tog, *k14, sl1, k2tog, psso; rep from * to last 17sts, k to last 3sts, ssk, k1. (63sts, with 8sts dec'd)

Row 4: Using Yarn A, knit.

Outer-section decreases

Row 1: Using Yarn A, k1, k2tog, *k12, sl1, k2tog, psso; rep from * to last 15sts, k to last 3sts, ssk, k1. (55sts, with 8sts dec'd)

Row 2: Using Yarn A, purl.

The previous 2 rows set the outer-section decrease pattern, with 2sts fewer being worked between decreases on every subsequent RS row.

Next, work these 2 rows another two times. (39sts after final row 2 has been completed)

Contrast stripe

Row 1 (RS): Using Yarn B, work as outer-section-decreases row 1. (31sts, with 8sts dec'd)

Row 2 (WS): Using Yarn B, knit.

Inner-section decreases

Row 1 (RS): Using Yarn A, work as outer-section-decreases row 1. (23sts, with 8sts dec'd)

Row 2 (WS): Using Yarn A, p1, p2tog, *p2, sl1, p2tog, psso; rep from * to last 5sts, p to last 3sts, p2tog-tbl, p1. (15sts, with 8sts dec'd)

Row 3: Using Yarn A, k1, p2tog, *sl1, p2tog, psso; rep from * to last 3sts, p2tog-tbl, p1. 8sts dec'd. (7sts, with 8sts dec'd)

Row 4: Using Yarn A, p1, p2tog, p1, p2tog-tbl, p1. (5sts, with 2sts dec'd)

Row 5: Using Yarn A, k2tog, sl1, k2tog, psso. (3sts, with 2sts dec'd)

Row 6: Using Yarn A, p3tog. (1st, with 2sts dec'd)

Fasten off, leaving a long enough yarn tail to sew centre-to-edge seam. Sew seam to complete the square.

To extend this swatch into a larger square shape, cast on the same number of additional stitches for each side of the square. Note that the side stitches are worked between the decreases; for the sample swatch, on row 1, each side has sixteen stitches between each decrease. Next, work as many additional outer-section right-side-row decreases as necessary to decrease the additional stitches before completing the square with the inner-section decreases worked on every row.

Step 5: Take the needle tip under the working yarn from front to back to create a yarn over. (3sts, with 1st inc'd)

Repeat Steps 3–5 until the required number of stitches have been made, ensuring that you end by working Step 4.

Place these stitches on to the working needles as required and, if working in the round, place a marker to indicate the beginning of the round. Begin the pattern and, after a few rows or rounds have been worked, close the centre loop by gently pulling on the tail end of the yarn.

Step 4 of the centre-start centre-loop method.

Step 5 of the centre-start centre-loop method.

Additional stitches are worked by repeating the relevant steps in sequence, until the necessary number of stitches are present.

Square with Multiple Increase Lines

Swatch information

Increases: M1 for knitted-flat swatch; yo for knitted-in-the-round swatch

Decreases: None

Start: Centre loop

Centre: Increase to outer edge

End: Outer edges of square

Border (outer edge): Garter stitch

Swatch instructions – working flat

Set-up

Using the smaller or larger needles, as preferred, and Yarn A, cast on 5sts by using the centre-loop method.

Row 1 (WS): Purl.

Row 2 (RS): Using Yarn A, *k1, m1; rep from * to last st, k1. (9sts, with 4sts inc'd)

Row 3: Using Yarn A, purl.

Row 4: Using Yarn A, work as row 2. (17sts, with 8sts inc'd)

Row 5: Using Yarn A, purl.

Inner-section increases

Row 1: Using Yarn A, k1, *m1, k3, m1, k1; rep from * to end. (25sts, with 8sts inc'd)

Row 2: Using Yarn A, purl.

The previous 2 rows set the inner-section-increases pattern, with an additional 2sts being worked between increases on every subsequent RS row. Next, work these 2 rows once. (33sts, with 8sts inc'd)

Contrast stripe

Row 1 (RS): Using Yarn B, work as inner-section-increases row 1. (41sts, with 8sts inc'd)

Row 2 (WS): Using Yarn B, knit.

Outer-section increases

Row 1 (RS): Using Yarn A, work as inner-section-increases row 1. (49sts, with 8sts inc'd)

Row 2 (WS): Using Yarn A, purl.

The previous 2 rows set the outer-section increases pattern, with an additional 2sts being worked

Square with multiple increase lines swatch, knitted flat with 3.5mm needles and baa ram ewe Titus 4ply yarn.

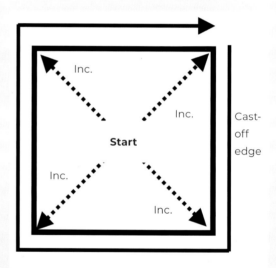

Diagram of square with multiple increase lines.

between increases on every subsequent RS row. Next, work these 2 rows another two times. (65sts after final row 2 has been completed)

Outer border

Row 1 (RS): Using Yarn A, work as inner-section-increases row 1. (73sts, with 8sts inc'd)

Row 2 (WS): Using Yarn A, knit.

Row 3: Using Yarn A, work as inner-section-increases row 1. (81sts, with 8sts inc'd)

Cast off knitwise with WS facing, leaving a long enough yarn tail to sew centre-to-edge seam. Sew seam to complete the square.

To extend this swatch into a larger square shape, continue increasing as set by the outer-section increases until the desired size is achieved.

Swatch instructions – working in the round

Note: One stitch marker and a set of five short double-pointed needles or one circular needle of a suitable length to accommodate all of the stitches are required for the working of this swatch.

Set-up
Using the smaller or larger needles, as preferred, and Yarn A, cast on 4sts by using the centre-loop method.
Place a stitch marker at the start of the round, and join to work in the round.
Round 1: Using Yarn A, knit.
Round 2: Using Yarn A, *k1, yo; rep from * to mrk. (8sts, with 4sts inc'd)
Round 3: Using Yarn A, purl.
Round 4: Using Yarn A, work as round 1. (16sts, with 8sts inc'd)
Round 5: Using Yarn A, purl.

Inner-section increases
Round 1: Using Yarn A, *k1, m1, k3, m1; rep from * to mrk. (24sts, with 8sts inc'd)
Round 2: Using Yarn A, knit.
The previous 2 rounds set the inner-section increases pattern, with an additional 2sts being worked between increases on every subsequent alternate round.
Next, work these 2 rounds another two times. (40sts after final row 2 has been completed)

Contrast stripe
Round 1: Using Yarn B, work as inner-section-increases round 1. (48sts, with 8sts inc'd)
Round 2: Using Yarn B, purl.

Square with multiple increase lines swatch, knitted in the round with 3.5mm needles and baa ram ewe Titus 4ply yarn.

Outer-section increases
Round 1: Using Yarn A, work as inner-section-increases round 1. (56sts, with 8sts inc'd)
Round 2: Using Yarn A, knit.
The previous 2 rounds set the outer-section increases pattern, with an additional 2sts being worked between increases on every subsequent alternate round.
Next, work these 2 rounds once. (64sts, with 8sts inc'd)

Outer border
Round 1: Using Yarn A, work as inner-section-increases round 1. (72sts, with 8sts inc'd)
Round 2: Using Yarn A, purl.
Round 3: Using Yarn A, work as inner-section-increases round 1. (80sts, with 8sts inc'd)
Cast off purlwise.

To extend this swatch into a larger square shape, continue increasing as set by the outer-section increases until the desired size is achieved.

Square-Shawl Design Development

This section has looked at different construction methods for square shapes. These squares can be used individually or in combination and can be scaled up to create complete shawl designs. The squares can also be combined on different scales to form new composite shawl shapes. The effect of pattern placement has also been considered through the inclusion of a contrast stripe. When combining a number of squares, pattern placement can be used for dramatic effect, for example, by combining single and multiple decrease squares. Individual squares can be joined by picking up stitches from the edge of an existing square and including these stitches in the cast on for a subsequent square.

One method used to visualize these combinations is a digital cut-and-paste or photomontage technique. Using images of the swatches, different combinations can be tested for layout combinations. This method can be carried out by using hand-drawn sketches, photographs of swatches placed into a spreadsheet or other software, or cutting out square shapes and laying them out in different orders. By reproducing one image of one swatch multiple times, whole shawl designs can be designed and tested before casting on and knitting the project. Remember that different scales can also be used and that not all squares in a shawl need to be of the same size. Some suggested layouts are proposed in the accompanying image and include multiple squares placed in different combinations.

These combinations have been illustrated using the example of the square with multiple decrease lines. As this square construction begins with the cast-on edges, part of the cast-on can include one or more sides of previous squares. Experimenting with shapes in this way can spark a whole new series of designs. Adding in different stitch patterns, yarn fibres and colours results in almost endless possibilities. I strongly encourage you to experiment and, most importantly, have fun!

Shawl-layout proposals

Proposal 1: A single square.

Proposal 2: Two or more squares worked side by side in a row, forming a rectangle as the overall shape. The properties of the square shapes have been maintained in the component parts of the larger rectangle.

Proposal 3: Four squares joined to form a larger square. This constructed square can be further extended in all directions, creating an even larger square or a rectangle.

Proposal 4: An odd number of squares, three or more, can be worked at different angles, with the centre square appearing as a diamond and the outer squares forming rectangles or wings.

OPPOSITE: Photomontage of shawl-layout proposals, featuring an image of a single square in different combinations.

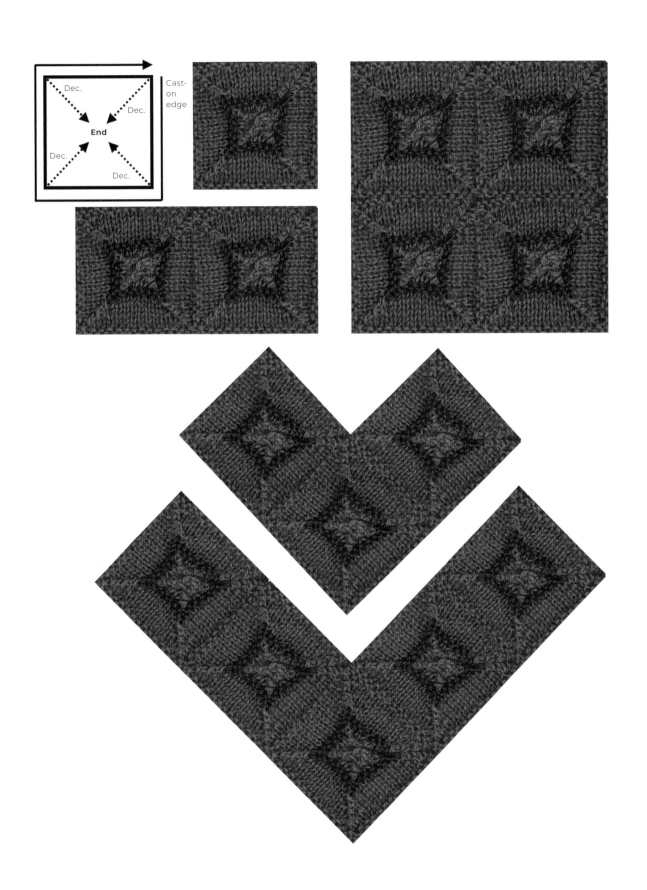

CHAPTER 5

RECTANGLES

Rectangles are very similar to squares; they are both flat shapes with four straight sides and four equal interior right angles. However, although all squares are rectangles, not all rectangles are squares. A more accurate description of a rectangle is a shape that has opposite sides of the same length. This opens up many possibilities for creative shawl designs.

A rectangle shape in shawl design can be used in several ways: as the overall shape, as one component part of a shawl, in combination with other rectangles or shapes, or as a rectangle that itself is made up of other shapes. For example, two or three squares can be combined end to end to form a larger rectangular shape that has two sets of two sides of equal length. One set of sides will be much longer than the other set. Another example is where two triangles are aligned along their long edges to create a rectangle shape.

Rectangular shawls can also be worn in many different ways, elegantly demonstrated by the featured beautifully illustrated page from the February 1926 edition of the magazine *Art - Goût - Beauté, Feuillets de l'élégance féminine*, from the Rijksmuseum online collection. Whether wrapped, draped or twisted around the neck, arms or body, a rectangular shawl can be an incredibly versatile fashion garment, as well as a simple, effective source of warmth.

OPPOSITE: Rectangular doorway, Lisbon, Portugal.

The length of the long edges of the rectangle can determine how many ways the shawl can be worn. An extremely long-sided rectangle could be wrapped around the neck and shoulders many times. A short-sided, wide rectangle can be draped as one length without lengthwise wraps of twists. As with the square-shawl examples, the choice of yarn and fibre can have a large impact on any rectangular-shawl design. Folding a rectangular shape knitted in very fine yarn could obscure the stitch pattern but can create warm, dense layers of knitted fabric. A rectangular shawl knitted in a heavier-weight yarn could result in extremely bulky folds, which could be difficult to wear under a coat or jacket but have wonderful dramatic impact.

Depending on the method of construction used and the corresponding stitch-pattern placement, this shape of shawl can reveal or hide different sections of stitch patterning. For example, if a long, narrow shawl knitted from short edge to short edge is to be worn wrapped around the neck multiple times, the most visible sections will be the two ends of the shawl. Focusing the most intricate pattern detail at these points creates maximum design impact. The orientation of a stitch pattern within a rectangle can be changed by using a different knitted construction. Working a rectangular shawl on the bias creates a knitted fabric with beautiful drape. A striped pattern knitted on the bias will appear as diagonal lines.

Inspiration for rectangular shapes and patterns can be found all around us, with doorways and windows providing many ready-made rectangular outlines and frames. The accompanying image shows a beautiful doorway in Lisbon, Portugal. As well as being a rectangular shape, this particular doorway is also made up of smaller rectangular panels. This doorway demon-

Illustration by A. Gillier from *Art - Goût - Beauté, Feuillets de l'élégance féminine (Février 1926, No. 66, 6e Année, p. 5)*, Rijksmuseum online collection (http://hdl.handle.net/10934/RM0001.COLLECT.508401).

Information for First Three Swatches of this Section

Swatch shape: Rectangle
Test yarn shown: baa ram ewe Titus 4ply (50-per-cent Wensleydale wool, 20-per-cent Bluefaced Leicester wool, 30-per-cent British alpaca, 320m/350yd per 100g hank)
Yarn A: Shade 007 (Aire); 1 × 100g skein, approximately 10g required for swatch
Yarn B: Shade 008 (Coal); 1 × 100g skein, less than 5g required for swatch
Needles (smaller size): A pair 3.25mm (UK 10/US 3) knitting needles
Needles (larger size): A pair 3.5mm (UK 9–10/US 4) knitting needles

strates that multiple inspirations can be found at dif-ferent scales within a single source. In this case, a shawl design could be inspired by one of the door panels or from the whole doorway. The beautiful surrounding tiles can also impact the design deci-sions taken. These multiple inspirations can be used together to develop a series of related stitch pat-terns for use within a single shawl. They can also be used to develop designs for several separate yet related shawls, as part of a collection. The sample swatches at the beginning of this section are inspired by this beautiful doorway. Each small swatch can be used as a starting point for new design develop-ments.

Rectangles Worked Edge to Edge

The edge-to-edge rectangle is constructed in a similar way to the edge-to-edge square. However, there are two additional considerations. The long edges of the rectangle shape can be formed either by stitches or by rows. Making a choice between the two depends on the preferred pattern placement.

Horizontally knitted lines of pattern or colour within both construction methods have the appearance of straight lines. The difference in orientation of these straight lines occurs when the rectangle is worn. The lines will appear as long vertical lines on a rectangle that has wider cast-on and -off edges and shorter side edges. The same horizontally knitted lines would have the appearance of short horizontal lines if the rectan-gle is knitted with narrow cast-on and -off edges, with the longer length occurring along the side edges. As in previous square examples, stitch patterns can be added on predetermined rows, using a wide variety of techniques. These may affect the tension and there-fore the number of rows to be worked. Edging patterns can be knitted on as the shape is being formed or added as an additional border after the knitting is complete.

For both options, a defined number of stitches are cast on, and rows are worked until the sides are shorter or longer than the cast-on edge. Once the desired length is reached, the stitches are cast off. The cast-on and -off edges will be of the same width and the two side edges will be of the same length.

The advantage of these methods of making a rectangle is that they are straightforward to make the calculations for, and it is easy to measure the different components. Once the desired length of the shorter and longer edges have been determined, the corres-ponding number of stitches and rows can be calcu-lated from a tension swatch. Edge-to-edge rectangles can be knitted using only knit and purl stitches, and no increasing or decreasing is necessary.

The following two example swatches show the proportional differences in the two methods. A short-edge-to-short-edge rectangle will have longer vertical length and narrower horizontal bands. The cast-on and -off borders are relatively far apart, as the full length of the rectangle is between them. For the long-edge-to-long-edge example, the vertical length is shorter.

However, the horizontal patterning is relatively much wider. The cast-on and -off borders appear closer together, and this should be taken into consideration when adding any additional stitch patterns. These aspects are especially important when multiple stitch patterns are combined.

Rectangle Worked Long Edge to Long Edge

Swatch information
Inspiration: Decorative doorway surrounded by ceramic tiles, Lisbon, Portugal
Increases: None
Decreases: None
Start: Cast-on long edge of rectangle

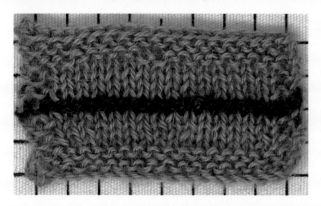

Long edge to long edge rectangle swatch, knitted with 3.25mm and 3.5mm needles and baa ram ewe Titus 4ply yarn.

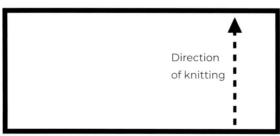

Diagram of a rectangle worked long edge to long edge.

Centre: Work in pattern, forming shorter edges of rectangle
End: Cast-off long edge of rectangle
Border (bottom, top and side edges): Garter stitch

Swatch instructions
Note: Throughout the swatch, the first stitch of every row is slipped, to create a neat selvedge.

Lower border
Using the smaller needles and Yarn A, cast on 19sts.
Knit 4 rows, slipping the first stitch of every row.
Change to using the larger needles.

Lower swatch section
Row 1 and every following RS row: Using Yarn A, sl1, k to end.
Row 2 and every following WS row: Using Yarn A, sl1, k1, p to last 2sts, k2.
The previous 2 rows set the lower-swatch-section pattern.
Next, work these 2 rows once.

Contrast stripe
Row 1 (RS): Using Yarn B, sl1, k to end.
Row 2 (WS): Using Yarn B, sl1, k to end.

Upper swatch section
Rows 1–4: Using Yarn A, work as lower-swatch-section rows 1–2.

Upper border
Change to using the smaller needles.
Using Yarn A, knit 4 rows, slipping the first stitch of every row.
Cast off knitwise.

To extend this swatch into a larger rectangle shape, cast on additional stitches and then work additional rows as required, ensuring that the sides form the shorter edges of the shape.

Rectangle Worked Short Edge to Short Edge

Swatch information

Inspiration: Decorative doorway surrounded by ceramic tiles, Lisbon, Portugal

Increases: None

Decreases: None

Start: Cast-on short edge of rectangle

Centre: Work in pattern, forming longer edges of rectangle

End: Cast-off short edge of rectangle

Border (bottom, top and side edges): Garter stitch

Swatch instructions

Note: Throughout the swatch, the first stitch of every row is slipped, to create a neat selvedge.

Lower border

Using the smaller needles and Yarn A, cast on 19sts. Knit 4 rows, slipping the first stitch of every row. Change to using the larger needles.

Lower swatch section

Row 1 and every following RS row: Using Yarn A, sl1, k to end.

Row 2 and every following WS row: Using Yarn A, sl1, k1, p to last 2sts, k2.

The previous 2 rows set the lower-swatch-section pattern.

Next, work these 2 rows another eight times.

Contrast stripe

Row 1 (RS): Using Yarn B, sl1, k to end.

Row 2 (WS): Using Yarn B, sl1, k to end.

Upper swatch section

Rows 1–10: Using Yarn A, work as lower-swatch-section rows 1–2.

Upper border

Change to using the smaller needles.

Using Yarn A, knit 4 rows, slipping the first stitch of every row.

Cast off knitwise.

To extend this swatch into a larger rectangle shape, cast on additional stitches and then work additional rows as required, ensuring that the sides form the longer edges of the shape.

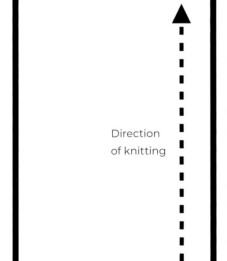

Cast-off edge

Direction of knitting

Cast-on edge

Diagram of a rectangle worked short edge to short edge.

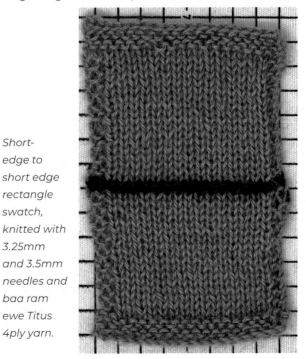

Short-edge to short edge rectangle swatch, knitted with 3.25mm and 3.5mm needles and baa ram ewe Titus 4ply yarn.

Rectangle with Two Decrease Lines

This rectangle is worked in a similar way to the mitred-corner square shape with a single decrease line. For this shape, two lines of double decreases are worked to create a rectangle. The number of stitches to be cast on is determined by the length of three sides of the rectangle. The rectangle is then knitted in rows, with decreases worked on each side of two corner stitches. The shape is completed by decreasing to a central point.

The calculation for the placement of the decrease lines depends on the length of the three sides of the rectangle. In the example shown, there are two short sides and one long side. The long side of the cast-on will equal the length of the opposite side of the rectangle that is created by knitting in rows. The decreases in this shape can be worked as a decora-tive feature, as they will run diagonally towards the top centre of the rectangle. Allowance must be made for accelerated decreases towards the central point, to balance the shape. Horizontal knitted rows of pattern-ing worked within this con- struction method will follow the angles of three sides of the rectangle, creat-ing a 'U' shape.

Rectangle Worked Point to Point and Partially on the Bias

Knitting a rectangular shape on the bias provides the opportunity to create a knitted fabric with beautiful drape and interesting patterning. This construction method starts in a similar way to the point-to-point square example. This technique is particularly effect-ive for stripes, as they appear diagonal in the finished

---

Rectangle with Two Decrease Lines

Swatch information

Inspiration: Decorative doorway surrounded by ceramic tiles, Lisbon, Portugal

Increases: None

Decreases: Sl1, k2tog, psso; sl1, p2tog, psso

Start: Cast-on stitches for three outer edges

Centre: Two sets of decreases worked to create rectangle shape

End: Centre of top edge

Border (cast-on edge and short sides): Garter stitch
Border (top edge): Garter stitch

Swatch instructions

Set-up

Using the smaller or larger needles, as preferred, and Yarn A, cast on 78sts.

Row 1 (RS): Using Yarn A, k18, sl1, k2tog, psso, k36, sl1, k2tog, psso, k to end. (74sts, with 4sts dec'd)

Row 2 (WS): Using Yarn A, knit.

Row 3: Using Yarn A, k17, sl1, k2tog, psso, k34, sl1,

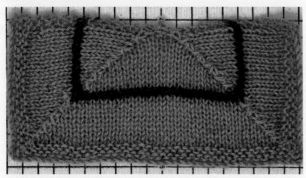

Two decrease lines rectangle swatch, knitted with 3.5mm needles and baa ram ewe Titus 4ply yarn.

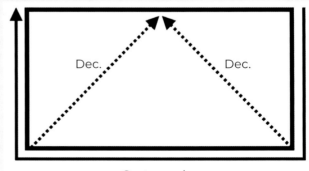

Cast-on edge

Diagram of a rectangle with two decrease lines.

knitting. An excellent inspirational source for striped bias rectangles are stairs with patterned or coloured edges. Photographing or sketching these stairs at an angle can help decide on the placement of the pattern stripes.

A bias-knitted rectangle begins with a single stitch. Stitches are then increased at each end of every right-side row until the desired width is reached. After this

A series of steps at the Barbican Estate, London, UK, photographed at an angle.

k2tog, psso, k to end. (70sts, with 4sts dec'd)
Row 4: Using Yarn A, knit.

Lower-section decreases
Row 1: Using Yarn A, k16, sl1, k2tog, psso, k32, sl1, k2tog, psso, k to end. (66sts, with 4sts dec'd)
Row 2: Using Yarn A, k2, p to last 2sts, k2.
The previous 2 rows set the lower-section decreases pattern; on each subsequent RS row, work 1st fewer before the first decrease and after the second decrease and 2sts fewer between the first and second decreases.
Next, work these 2 rows another four times. (50sts after final row 2 has been completed)

Contrast stripe
Row 1 (RS): Using Yarn B, work as lower-section-decreases row 1. (46sts, with 4sts dec'd)
Row 2 (WS): Using Yarn B, knit.

Upper-section decreases
Rows 1–4: Using Yarn A, work as lower-section-decreases rows 1–2. (38sts, after row 4 has been completed)

Row 5: Using Yarn A, work as lower-section-decreases row 1. (34sts, with 4sts dec'd)
Row 6: Using Yarn A, k2, p5, sl1, p2tog, psso, p14, sl1, p2tog, psso, p to last 2sts, k2. (30sts, with 4sts dec'd)
The previous 2 rows set the upper-section decreases pattern; on each subsequent row, work 1st fewer before the first decrease and after the second decrease and 2sts fewer between the first and second decreases.
Next, work these 2 rows another four times. (10sts after final row has been completed)

Centre
Row 1 (RS): Using Yarn A, k1, sl1, k2tog, psso, k2, sl1, k2tog, psso, k1. (6sts, with 4sts dec'd)
Row 2 (WS): Using Yarn A, k2tog three times. (3sts, with 3sts dec'd)
Row 3: Using Yarn A, sl1, k2tog, psso. (1st, with 2sts dec'd)
Fasten off.

point, stitches are decreased at the beginning and increased at the end of every right-side row. Working balanced decreases and increases in this way keeps the width of the rectangle constant. The side edges remain straight. Once the desired length is reached, stitches are decreased at both ends of every right-side row until a single stitch remains. The decreases will increase in frequency towards the final point of the

Rectangle Worked Point to Point and Partially on the Bias

Swatch information
Inspiration: Stairs, Barbican Estate, London, UK
Increases: M1l, m1r
Decreases: K2tog, ssk
Start: Point of lower rectangle
Centre: Knitted on the bias
End: Point of upper rectangle
Border (outer edges): Garter stitch
Test yarn shown: baa ram ewe Titus 4ply (50-per-cent Wensleydale wool, 20-per-cent Bluefaced Leicester wool, 30-per-cent British alpaca, 320m/350yd per 100g hank)
Yarn A: Shade 003 (Parkin); 1 × 100g skein, approximately 10g required for swatch
Yarn B: Shade 008 (Coal); 1 × 100g skein, less than 5g required for swatch
Needles: A pair 3.5mm (UK 9–10/US 4) knitting needles

Swatch instructions
Note: For striped bias section, carry yarn not in use up side of work, twisting yarns together at the beginning of every RS row.

Lower point
Using 3.5mm needles and Yarn A, cast on 1st.
Row 1 (RS): Using Yarn A, k1, p1, k1 all into same st. (3sts, with 2sts inc'd)
Row 2 (WS): Using Yarn A, knit.
Row 3: Using Yarn A, k1, m1r, k to last st, m1l, k1. (5sts, with 2sts inc'd)
Row 4: Using Yarn A, knit.

Increase pattern
Row 1 (RS): Using Yarn A, k1, m1r, k to last st, m1l, k1. (7sts, with 2sts inc'd)

Row 2 and every following WS row: Using Yarn A, k2, p to last 2sts, k2.
The previous 2 rows set the increase pattern.
Next, work these 2 rows another five times. (17sts after final row 2 has been completed)

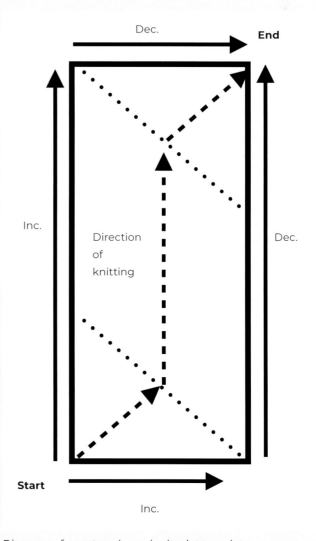

Diagram of a rectangle worked point to point.

rectangle in order to complete the shape evenly. The two short sides of this bias-knitted rectangle will be of the same length, as will be the two long sides. Edging patterns can be knitted in as the shape is being formed or added on after the knitting is completed. Placement of integral or edging stitch patterns must take into account the required stitch increases and decreases at each end of the row.

Contrast stripe
Row 1 (RS): Using Yarn B, work as increase-pattern row 1. (19sts, with 2sts inc'd)
Row 2 (WS): Using Yarn B, knit.

Bias pattern with contrast stripes
Row 1 (RS): Using Yarn A, k1, ssk, k to last st, m1l, k1.
Row 2 (WS): Using Yarn A, k2, p to last 2sts, k2.
Rows 3–4: Using Yarn A, work as rows 1–2.
Row 5: Using Yarn B, k1, ssk, k to last st, m1l, k1.
Row 6: Using Yarn B, knit.
The previous 6 rows set the bias pattern.
Next, work these 6 rows another two times.

Decrease pattern
Row 1 (RS): Using Yarn A, k1, ssk, k to last 3sts, k2tog, k1. (17sts, with 2sts dec'd)
Row 2 (WS): Using Yarn A, k2, p to last 2sts, k2.
The previous 2 rows set the decrease pattern.
Next, work these 2 rows another two times. (13sts after final row 2 has been completed)

Upper point
Row 1 (RS): Using Yarn A, work as decrease-pattern row 1. (11sts, with 2sts dec'd)
Row 2 (WS): Using Yarn A, k1, ssk, p to last 3sts, k2tog, k1. (9sts, with 2sts dec'd)
Rows 3–4: Using Yarn A, work as rows 1–2. (5sts, after row 4 has been completed)
Row 5: Using Yarn A, k1, sl1, k2tog, psso. (3sts, with 2sts dec'd)
Row 6: Using Yarn A, sl1, k2tog, psso. (1st, with 2sts dec'd)
Fasten off.

Point to point and partially on the bias rectangle swatch, knitted with 3.5mm needles and baa ram ewe Titus 4ply yarn.

Rectangular-Shawl Design Development

This section has considered several different examples of knitted rectangles. An individual rectangle is a very flexible and adaptable shape for a shawl. A knitting pattern for a rectangular shawl, after due consideration of the surrounding borders, can be very straightforward to design, as shown for the Agora-Pattern swatch in the edgings section of this book (*see* Chapter 3). In the Agora swatch example, the cast-on border was worked first. A garter-stitch ridge pattern was selected for the main-shawl body. The side-edging patterns were worked at the beginning and end of every main-section row. The edgings and the garter-stitch ridge pattern were repeated until the desired length was reached. The swatch was then completed with the cast-off border.

The orientation of the stitch pattern can be altered in a rectangular shawl by using different construction methods. For example, two squares or rectangles worked from the centre of the shawl outwards will form an overall rectangle shape. The stitch patterns within this shape will be mirror-imaged, that is, worked in the opposite direction from each other. Another example is where an additional shape is placed in the centre of two rectangles. This extends the length of the shawl and adds a multidirectional stitch-pattern element to the design. This type of shape combination is explored for the Riverside Shawl (*see* Chapter 9). The Riverside design starts with a central-square shape and extends into two outer rectangle shapes with mirror-imaged stitch patterns.

OPPOSITE: Rectangular Riverside Shawl with multidirectional stitch patterns. (Photographed by Maxine Vining.)

CHAPTER 6

TRIANGLES

A triangle shape is a shape with three straight sides. There are several different types of triangle, each defined by their internal angles and the lengths of their sides. Names of triangles include equilateral, isosceles, right-angled, scalene and obtuse. Many triangles can be knitted by using increases or decreases, or both, to create the shape. For example, a right-angled triangle can be created by beginning with a single stitch and increasing stitches on one side of every right-side row until the desired width is reached. This type of triangle can also be formed by starting at the wide edge and decreasing on one side of every right-side row until a single stitch remains. The choice of method depends on other factors such as choice of stitch pattern, inclusion of edgings and the amount of yarn available.

All three sides of an equilateral-triangle shawl will be of the same length. However, it is some of the asymmetric properties of triangles that make them excellent bases for shawl design. The addition of a stitch pattern to a right-angled-triangle shawl shape can distort the shape and create interesting effects. Therefore, by using the properties of triangle shapes, a wide variety of interesting shawl shapes can be designed. Some well-known shapes include those given in the following list of types of triangles. However, shawl designs do not need to conform to these parameters; these triangle types are listed only to provide ideas and suggest possibilities.

OPPOSITE: Isosceles triangles on the side of the right-angle-shaped Leadenhall Building, commonly known as the Cheesegrater, City of London, UK.

List of triangle types

Equilateral triangle: this has three equal sides and always has three equal angles of 60 degrees in each corner.
Isosceles triangle: this can have two equal sides and two equal angles or two acute angles and one obtuse angle.
Obtuse triangle: this has three different angles, none of the sides are equal in length and one angle is greater than 90 degrees.
Right-angled triangle: this has one 90-degree angle. It can also be an isosceles triangle with angles of 90, 45 and 45 degrees.
Scalene triangle: this has three different angles and none of the sides are equal in length.

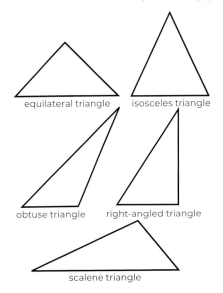

Triangle shapes.

La cape ecossaise, illustration by G. Calderon, from Gazette du Bon Ton. Art – Modes & Frivolités *(1914, 2e Année, No. 4), Rijksmuseum online collection (https://www.rijksmuseum.nl/en/collection/RP-P-2009-1937-2).*

The opening image of this chapter shows an example of an excellent inspirational source for triangle shapes. The photograph shows buildings in the City of London, UK. The most prominent feature is the Leadenhall Building, also known as the Cheesegrater, which was designed by the architects of the firm Rogers Stirk Harbour + Partners. As well as the main shape of the building being triangular, a series of smaller isosceles triangles are located on the side. This combination of multiple triangles in one inspirational image can lead to many shawl-design possibilities and demonstrates the rich source of inspirations in the urban environment.

Triangular shawls can be worn in multiple ways: folded, unfolded, wrapped or draped. The length of the longest edge of the triangle shawl can often determine

Information Common to All Swatches in this Section

Inspiration: Leadenhall Building, City of London, UK
Swatch shape: Triangle
Test yarn shown: baa ram ewe Titus 4ply (50-per-cent Wensleydale wool, 20-per-cent Bluefaced Leicester wool, 30-per-cent British alpaca, 320m/350yd per 100g hank)
Yarn A: Shade 007 (Aire); 1 × 100g skein, approximately 10g required for swatch
Yarn B: Shade 001 (White Rose); 1 × 100g skein, less than 5g required for swatch
Needles: A pair 3.5mm (UK 9–10/US 4) knitting needles

how many ways the shawl can be worn, as this length provides the edge that wraps the furthest distance. The addition of fringing and embellishment can create a dramatic effect. The accompanying illustration from The *Gazette du Bon Ton* from 1914 shows a wonderful example of a dramatic, draped triangular-shaped shawl.

This section considers methods and techniques to make several different triangle shapes. Each method can be used to test yarns and stitch patterns, and can be scaled up to make a larger shape.

Isosceles Triangles

There are several ways to knit an isosceles triangle with two equal sides. In this section, two main methods are considered: a point-to-cast-off-edge method and a tab-to-point method.

Point-to-cast-off-edge method

The point-to-cast-off-edge method of creating a triangle begins with a single stitch. Stitches are then increased at each end of every right-side row, or on a regularly spaced predetermined number of rows, until the desired width is reached, when the stitches are then cast off. Increases are made by using a yarn over or paired increases such as m1l and m1r. The choice of increase method will depend on the main stitch pattern worked within the shawl body. For example, an openwork stitch pattern will look good with yarn-over increases. Adding a stitch pattern to this construction method can alter the length and width of the triangle sides. A test swatch will show the effect of any patterning. Horizontally knitted stitch patterns worked within this construction method will have the appearance of a horizontal line. Depending on the orientation of wear of the triangular shawl, this line may appear in a different orientation.

In most cases, the two sides of the triangle with increases will be of the same length. The number of stitches at the cast-off end can be determined at the last moment, by continuing to increase until the desired width measurement is reached. An advantage of working this way is that the size of the triangle can be decided on as the stitches are being increased. If a limited amount of yarn is available, this method allows the knitter to continue to increase and grow the shawl until almost all of the yarn is used. This is especially useful if the borders and edgings are also knitted at the same time as the shawl body. Only enough yarn to

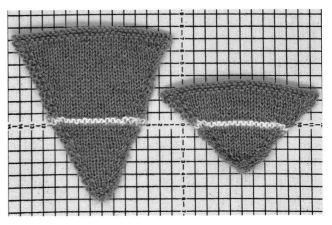

Comparison of point to cast-off edge isosceles triangle swatches (narrow on left and wide on right), knitted with 3.5mm needles and baa ram ewe Titus 4ply yarn.

work the final border edging needs to be retained after the shawl body is completed.

Depending on the frequency of the increases, different versions of these triangles can be made by using this technique. For example, a long, narrow triangle will be formed if the increases are spaced out over more rows, that is, for example, worked every four rows instead of every second row. Conversely, a wide triangle is formed if the increases are made on every row.

Isosceles Triangles Worked Point to Cast-Off Edge: Wide and Narrow Versions

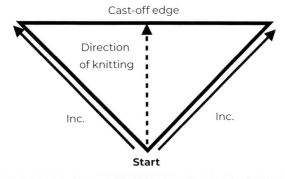

Diagram of an isosceles triangle (wide) worked point to cast-off edge.

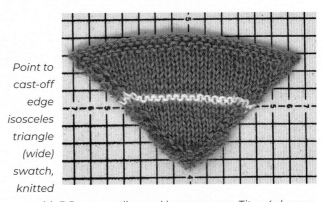

Point to cast-off edge isosceles triangle (wide) swatch, knitted with 3.5mm needles and baa ram ewe Titus 4ply yarn.

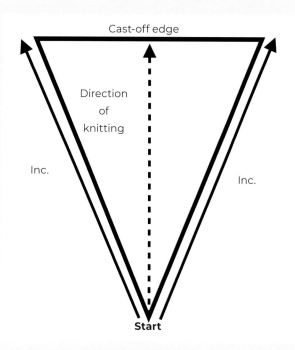

Diagram of isosceles triangle (narrow) worked point to cast-off edge.

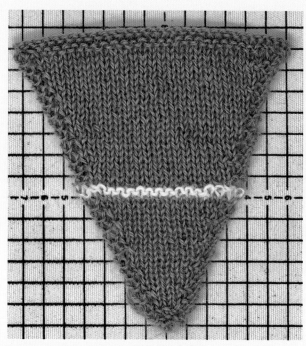

Point to cast-off edge isosceles triangle (narrow) swatch, knitted with 3.5mm needles and baa ram ewe Titus 4ply yarn.

Swatch information

Swatch shape: Isosceles triangle
Increases: M1l, m1r
Decreases: None
Start: Lower point of triangle
Centre: Increase pattern
End: Top edge of triangle
Border (outer and top edges): Garter stitch

Swatch instructions – wide triangle

Lower point

Using 3.5mm needles and Yarn A, cast on 1st.
Row 1 (RS): Using Yarn A, k1, p1, k1 all into same st. (3sts, with 2sts inc'd)
Row 2 (WS): Using Yarn A, knit.
Row 3: Using Yarn A, k1, m1r, k to last st, m1l, k1. (5sts, with 2sts inc'd)
Row 4: Using Yarn A, knit.

Lower increase section

Row 1 (RS): Using Yarn A, sl1, k1, m1r, k to last st, m1l, k1. (7sts, with 2sts inc'd)

Row 2 and every following WS row: Using Yarn A, sl1, k1, p to last 2sts, k2.
The previous 2 rows set the increase pattern.
Next, work these 2 rows another five times. (17sts after final row 2 has been completed)

Contrast stripe

Row 1 (RS): Using Yarn B, work as lower-increase-section row 1. (19sts, with 2sts inc'd)
Row 2 (WS): Using Yarn B, sl1, k to end.

Upper increase section

Rows 1–8: Using Yarn A, work as lower-increase-section rows 1–2. (27sts after final row 2 has been completed)

Upper border

Row 1 (RS): Using Yarn A, work as lower-increase-section row 1. (29sts, with 2sts inc'd)

Row 2 (WS): Using Yarn A, sl1, k to end.

Row 3: Using Yarn A, work as lower-increase-section row 1. (31sts, with 2sts inc'd)

Cast off knitwise.

Swatch instructions – narrow triangle
Lower point

Using 3.5mm needles and Yarn A, cast on 1st. Work as for lower point of wide triangle.

Lower increase section

Row 1 (RS): Using Yarn A, sl1, k1, m1r, k to last st, m1l, k1. (7sts, with 2sts inc'd)

Row 2 (WS): Using Yarn A, sl1, k1, p to last 2sts, k2.

Row 3: Using Yarn A, sl1, k1, k to last 2sts, k2.

Row 4: Using Yarn A, work as row 2.

The previous 4 rows set the increase pattern.

Next, work these 4 rows another four times. (15sts after final row 2 has been completed)

Next, work rows 1–2 once. (17sts after row 2 has been completed)

Contrast stripe

Row 1 (RS): Using Yarn B, work as lower-increase-section row 3.

Row 2 (WS): Using Yarn B, sl1, k to end.

Upper increase section

Rows 1–20: Using Yarn A, work as lower-increase-section rows 1–4. (27sts after final row 4 has been completed)

Upper border

Row 1 (RS): Using Yarn A, work as lower-increase-section row 1. (29sts, with 2sts inc'd)

Row 2 (WS): Using Yarn A, sl1, k to end.

Row 3: Using Yarn A, work as lower-increase-section row 1. (31sts, with 2sts inc'd)

Cast off knitwise.

Garter-tab-to-point method

The overall shape of this triangle is similar to the wide point-to-cast-off-edge triangle in the previous example. However, this shape actually consists of two linked triangles that are knitted at the same time. Four increases are worked across the row: at the beginning and end and on each side of the central spine. These increases grow both sides of the shawl at the same rate. The two sides of the shawl are often, but not always, identical. This creates a mirror-imaged pattern on each side of the central spine. This construction feature results in plenty of options to add decorative detail and to create interesting effects with stitch patterns.

Horizontally knitted patterning will appear as diagonal lines on the finished shawl. This construction method is useful where a limited amount of yarn is available, as the shawl can be increased and grown until almost all of the yarn is used, ensuring that enough yarn remains for the final cast-off.

The top-down method of creating a triangle usually begins with knitting a garter-stitch tab. This small length of knitting fills the notch that would otherwise be left at the top of the shawl. As previously described in the techniques section, tabs are often knitted in garter stitch, but they can be knitted in any stitch pattern, perhaps to match the surrounding edging or main stitch pattern. After picking up the stitches around the tab, additional stitches are then increased at each end of every right-side row and on each side of the central spine of the shawl. Once the desired centre depth is reached, the stitches are cast off, usually with a decorative border or edging being added.

Right-Angled Triangles

A right-angled triangle has one 90-degree angle. It can also be an isosceles triangle with angles of 90, 45 and 45 degrees. Right-angled triangles make interesting asymmetric shawl shapes, with different lengths for each side.

Isosceles Triangle Worked From Garter Tab to Point

Swatch information
Swatch shape: Isosceles triangle
Increase: M1
Decreases: None
Start: Garter-stitch tab
Centre: Increase pattern
End: Outer edge of triangle
Borders (start and cast-off edges): Garter stitch

Swatch instructions
Note: A stitch marker is required for the working of this swatch. The stitch marker is placed at the centre of the shawl and is used to help place the increase stitches. On subsequent rows after the placement of the marker, slip the marker from the left-hand needle to the right-hand needle as it is reached.
Note: Throughout the swatch, the first stitch of every row is slipped, to create a neat selvedge.

Set-up
Using 3.5mm needles and Yarn A, cast on 3sts. Knit 7 rows. After working the seventh row (RS), do not turn work.

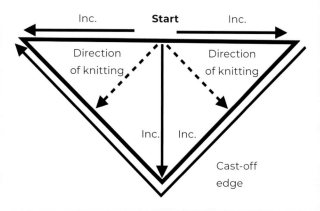

Diagram of triangle worked from garter tab to point.

Next, with 3sts on right-hand needle, pick up and knit 2sts along side of tab and 3sts along cast-on edge. (8sts)
Next row (WS): Sl1, k to end.

Increase section
Row 1 (RS, placing stitch marker): Using Yarn A, sl1, (k1, m1) twice, k1, pm, k1, (m1, k1) twice, k1. (12sts, with 4sts inc'd)
Row 2 (WS): Using Yarn A, sl1, k1, p to last 2sts, k2.
Row 3: Using Yarn A, sl1, k1, m1, k to 1st before mrk, m1, k2, m1, k to last 2sts, m1, k2. (16sts, with 4sts inc'd)
Row 4: Using Yarn A, work as row 2.
The previous 2 rows set the increase pattern.
Next, work these 2 rows another four times. (32sts after final row 4 has been completed)

Contrast-stripe section
Row 1 (RS): Using Yarn B, work as increase-section row 3. (36sts, with 4sts inc'd)
Row 2 (WS): Using Yarn B, sl1, k to end.
Rows 3–12: Using Yarn A, work as increase-section rows 3–4. (56sts after row 12 has been completed)

Border
Row 1 (RS): Using Yarn A, work as increase-section row 3. (60sts, with 4sts inc'd)
Row 2 (WS): Using Yarn A, sl1, k to end.
Row 3: Using Yarn A, work as increase-section row 3. (64sts, with 4sts inc'd)
Cast off knitwise.

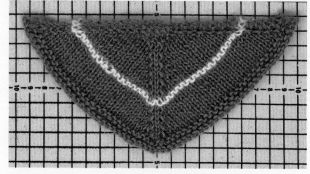

Centre start to point triangle swatch, knitted with 3.5mm needles and baa ram ewe Titus 4ply yarn.

Point-to-cast-off-edge method

The point-to-cast-off-edge method of creating a right-angled triangle begins with a single stitch, just like the first two examples of an isosceles triangle. However, stitches are then increased only at one end of every right-side row, or a regularly spaced predetermined number of rows, until the desired width is reached, when the stitches are then cast off.

In most cases, all three sides of this triangle will be of a different length, forming an asymmetric shawl shape. The actual lengths of the sides will depend on the stitch pattern used and the rate of stitch increase. The stitch-pattern tension will affect the width and length of the shape. The rate of increase will determine whether a shorter, wider shape or a longer, narrower shape is formed. The decision on whether to increase at the beginning or end of a row will depend on the main stitch pattern and the type of edging pattern chosen. Swatching for different options is the best way to decide which to choose.

As with the previous isosceles-triangle examples, this construction method is very useful if only a limited amount of yarn is available. After taking into account borders and edgings, the shawl can be grown until almost all of the yarn is used, leaving sufficient yarn for working only the final border.

A line of pattern worked horizontally within this shape can take on several different appearances, depending on which way round the final shawl triangle is orientated when worn. For example, with the long increase edge across the shoulders, the line of pattern will appear diagonally.

Adding Pattern to a Triangular-Shawl Swatch

The previous sections have considered the effect of a single line of pattern, represented by a garter-stitch stripe worked in a contrast shade of yarn. One of the most rewarding aspects of shawl design is being creative with stitch patterns. In this section, the image of the Leadenhall Building in the City of London provides new pattern inspiration for a more complex stitch pattern. The design process for adding a stitch pattern can be considered as a series of steps. These steps should be used as a guide, rather than as a fixed sequence. Adapt and add to them to suit your own personal preferences.

Planning the design

Step 1. Inspiration
Deciding on a stitch pattern can be daunting at first. However, returning to the original inspirational image for this section helps to define the choices. In this example, one of the main features of the Leadenhall Building is the series of small isosceles triangles on one side of the building. These triangles are orientated with the widest edge at the lower part of each triangle and the point at the top. Looking closely again, each triangle has two small right-angled triangles on each side of the narrowing section. It is these small triangles that inspire the pattern for this swatch.

Step 2. Stitch pattern
Translating this inspiration into a stitch pattern begins with capturing the essence of the shape in texture by using knit and purl stitches. There are two sections to the triangle pattern, one worked in stocking stitch and the other in reverse stocking stitch. These two sections provide contrast in the knitted fabric, with one part appearing smooth and the other ridged. Using this type of textured pattern has the advantage of creating a reversible design, and the right and wrong sides of the shawl will look similar.

Step 3. Shape
The choice of the overall shawl shape can also be found in the inspirational image. For this swatch, a right-angled-triangle shape most closely represents the overall shape of the Leadenhall Building. After the triangle tip is worked, this swatch has increases worked at one end of every right-side row.

Right-Angled Triangle Worked Point to Cast-Off Edge

Swatch information
Swatch shape: Right-angled triangle
Increase: M1
Decreases: None
Start: Point of triangle
Centre: Increase pattern
End: Cast-off border
Borders (inner, outer and cast-off edges): Garter stitch

Swatch instructions
Set-up
Using 3.5mm needles and Yarn A, cast on 1st.
Row 1 (RS): Using Yarn A, k1, p1, k1 all into same st. (3sts, with 2sts inc'd)
Row 2 (WS): Using Yarn A, knit.
Row 3: Using Yarn A, k to last st, m1, k1. (4sts, with 1st inc'd)
Row 4: Using Yarn A, knit.

Cast-off edge

Direction of knitting

Inc.

Start

Diagram of a right-angled triangle worked point to cast-off edge.

Lower increase section
Row 1 (RS): Using Yarn A, sl1, k to last 2sts, m1, k2. (5sts, with 1st inc'd)
Row 2 (WS): Using Yarn A, sl1, k1, p to last 2sts, k2.
Row 3: Using Yarn A, sl1, k1, k to end.
Rows 4–6: Using Yarn A, work as rows 2–3.
The previous 6 rows set the increase pattern.
Next, work these 6 rows another four times. (9sts after final row 6 has been completed)

Contrast-stripe section
Row 1 (RS): Using Yarn B, work as lower-increase-section row 1. (10sts, with 1st inc'd)
Row 2 (WS): Using Yarn B, sl1, k to end.
Rows 3–6: Using Yarn A, work as lower-increase-section rows 2–3.

Upper increase section
Next, work lower-increase-section rows 1–6 another three times. (13sts after final row 6 has been completed)

Upper border
Row 1 (RS): Using Yarn A, work as lower-increase-section row 1. (14sts, with 1st inc'd)
Row 2 (WS): Using Yarn A, sl1, k to end.
Row 3: Using Yarn A, work as lower-increase-section row 1. (15sts, with 1st inc'd)
Cast off knitwise.

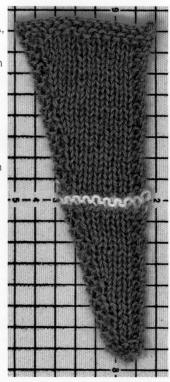

Right-angled triangle worked point to cast-off swatch, knitted with 3.5mm needles and baa ram ewe Titus 4ply yarn.

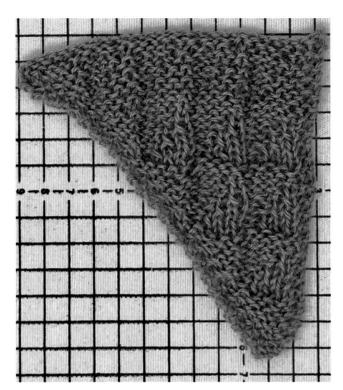

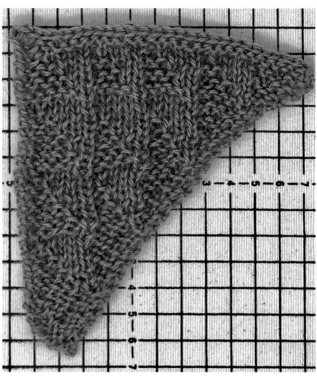

Textured Triangles swatch, right side showing, knitted with 3.5mm needles and baa ram ewe Titus 4ply yarn.

Textured Triangles swatch, wrong side showing, knitted with 3.5mm needles and baa ram ewe Titus 4ply yarn.

Step 4. Pattern repeat

When there are enough stitches, a textured-triangles stitch pattern can be introduced into the shape. As one stitch is increased every two rows, it therefore takes ten rows to create five new stitches. When deciding which stitch pattern is suitable for which shape, it can be helpful to think about how this stitch pattern will fit into the shawl increases. This can be calculated by using stitch and row multiples. In this example, the textured-triangles stitch pattern is five stitches wide and ten rows long. For every ten rows of swatch knitted, five new stitches are increased. One additional triangle stitch pattern repeat can therefore be added every ten rows, as there are five new stitches available. Using charting software such as Stitchmastery can help to visualize the proposed pattern with increases. Alternatively, drawing out the pattern with a pen or pencil on paper or graph paper or by using drawing software works really well. Making detailed notes, however they are recorded, is essential.

Step 5. Increases

At the same time as deciding how the stitch pattern fits into the shawl shape, the increases themselves also need to be considered. As discussed in previous sections, there are many different increase stitches to choose from. The increases can be decorative and can be matched to the rest of the stitch pattern. In this example, the increases are worked as m1. With five stitches increased over ten rows, the new stitches also require a stitch pattern until they are included in the main-swatch stitch pattern. In this case, the new stitches are worked in garter stitch. To create a unified design, garter stitch is also used for other framing sections of the swatch. These framing sections include the straight edge of the swatch and the initial increases required for the swatch point.

Step 6. Cast-off border

A wide variety of cast-off edging patterns can be used

to complete the swatch. To help decide on a suitable pattern, both the original inspiration and the stitch pattern from the other edges are considered. Based on this approach, the pattern for the cast-off border includes triangles worked on a garter-stitch background.

Creating the swatch

Step 1. Writing the pattern

Even though this is a small sample swatch, writing out the pattern in detail is an extremely important next step. By working this way, the swatch can easily be adapted and scaled up to a full shawl project. All of the key information is recorded and tested. A pattern can be written in many different ways, and each designer will have their preferred style. At this stage of the design development, the aim is to experiment and find a suitable method of recording ideas that can be referred to at a later date. This swatch pattern is written out in detail below and has charts of the textured-triangles stitch repeats. There are two stitch patterns: Pattern A is the main-swatch textured-triangles pattern; Pattern B is the cast-off-border garter-stitch textured-triangles pattern.

The set-up instructions from the right-angled triangle shown earlier in this section provide the pattern for the swatch point. As the textured-triangles stitch pattern is five stitches wide, the swatch point is increased until five stitches are available for use with the main pattern. In addition to the pattern stitches, there are border stitches to be included. The border is made up of two stitches at the beginning and end of every row. These stitches are worked in garter stitch throughout, with the first stitch of every row being slipped to form a neat edge. The swatch increase stitches are worked before the last two border stitches on every right-side row.

Step 2. Choosing the yarn

Try to select a yarn that reflects an aspect of the inspiration. For example, this could be related to the texture or the colour. For this swatch, the colour blue was the main factor. The pure-wool fibre also provides excellent stitch definition for the textured stitch pattern.

Step 3. Knitting the swatch

The ball bands of the majority of yarns provide guidance about the suitable size of needles to use to work the yarn. However, it is important to experiment, and a chosen stitch pattern may look much better when worked with a larger or smaller needle size than that suggested.

Step 4. Blocking the swatch

After the swatch has been knitted, block it according to the instructions on the ball band and by whichever means are to be used if the swatch is to be extended to a full shawl design. Using the same method is essential to test how the yarn, stitch pattern and swatch shape interact with the chosen blocking method.

Reviewing the design process

Once the swatch has been completed and blocked, an assessment can be made of all of the different aspects of the swatch. Overall, did the swatch work out as expected? If not, why not? What can be done to improve any aspect? Are there any changes that could be made to make it work even better? Thinking about what has worked well and what has not turned out as expected is a really important step before extending a design. Don't be afraid to make changes or alter the original plan. Of course, if a large number of changes are made, a new swatch will be required. Remember to update your notes with these findings.

Using this swatch as an example, there are several things that have worked really well. The contrast between the different stitch patterns shows the triangular structure very well. The garter-stitch increase edging pattern forms a pattern of small triangles, reflecting the main stitch pattern. The two-stitch edging has sufficient stretch on both sides of the shawl to maintain a well-defined border. The slipped stitch at the beginning of each row has created a neat edge. This swatch contains useful stitch-pattern information for initial design development. However, if this swatch were to be extended into a full-size shawl, several more pattern repeats would be required, as a larger swatch would be necessary from which to obtain accurate tension measurements.

To extend and experiment with the swatch, a different yarn could be used. A heavier-weight yarn, such as aran-weight, would make the individual stitches more prominent and create a bold structural pattern. The scale of the individual triangles could be changed by increasing the number of stitches and rows worked with Pattern A. For example, larger triangle shapes could be added as the shawl progresses, with these new stitch patterns worked over ten stitches and twenty rows. These larger shapes will still fit into the increase pattern of the shawl, with enough stitches increased over the new number of rows to add an additional repeat. The cast-off edging could also be extended over more rows, to make a more prominent feature of the shawl edge.

By using these swatch design steps as a guide, new ideas can be designed and tested for a wide variety of stitch patterns and shawl shapes. The order of the design steps can be changed to suit the project. For example, a border design may inspire a whole shawl and may require the most focus in design development. Working with individual shapes can help with this development. Understanding how a shawl shape is created allows patterns to be placed to maximum effect. Shawl swatches are like mini design sketches that a designer can work from again and again.

Adding Pattern to a Triangular Shawl Swatch

Swatch information
Swatch shape: Right-angled triangle
Increase: M1
Decreases: None
Start: Point of triangle
Centre: Increase pattern and Textured-Triangles patterns
End: Cast-off-border garter-stitch-triangles pattern
Borders: Garter stitch

Stitch patterns
Pattern A, worked over 5sts and 10 rows
Row 1 (RS): K4, p1.
Row 2 (WS): K1, p4.
Row 3: K3, p2.
Rows 4–5: K2, p3.
Row 6: K3, p2.
Row 7: K1, p4.
Row 8: K4, p1.
Row 9: Purl.
Row 10: Knit.

Pattern B, worked over 5sts and 8 rows
Row 1 (RS): K4, p1.
Row 2 and all WS rows: Knit.
Row 3: K3, p2.

Row 5: K2, p3.
Row 7: K1, p4.

Swatch instructions
Note: A stitch marker is required for the working of this swatch.
Use 3.5mm needles and Yarn A throughout.

Textured Triangles Pattern A chart.

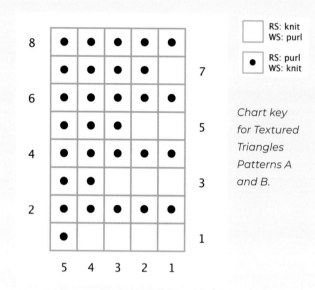

8 ● ● ● ● ●

● ● ● ● ● 7

6 ● ● ● ● ●

● ● ● 5

4 ● ● ● ● ●

● ● 3

2 ● ● ● ● ●

● 1

5 4 3 2 1

□ RS: knit
WS: purl

▣ RS: purl
WS: knit

Chart key for Textured Triangles Patterns A and B.

Textured Triangles Pattern B chart.

Set-up

Cast on 1st.

Row 1 (RS): K1, p1, k1 all into same st. (3sts, with 2sts inc'd)

Row 2 (WS): Knit.

Row 3: K1, (k1, p1, k1) all into next st, k1. (5sts, with 2sts inc'd)

Row 4: Sl1, k to end.

Increase section

Row 1 (RS): Sl1, k to last 2sts, m1, k2. (6sts, with 1st inc'd)

Row 2 (WS): Sl1, k1, p to last 2sts, k2.

The previous 2 rows set the increase pattern.

Next, work these 2 rows another four times. (9sts after final row 2 has been completed)

Explanatory note: There are now enough stitches for both edges and one repeat of Textured-Triangles

Pattern A to be worked. Refer to charted or written instructions for Pattern A as desired. A stitch marker is placed to show where Pattern A ends on the RS rows and where it begins on the WS rows. On subsequent rows, when the stitch marker is reached, slip it from the left-hand needle to the right-hand needle.

First pattern section

Row 1 (RS, placing stitch marker): Sl1, k1, work Pattern A row 1, pm, m1, k2. (10sts, with 1st inc'd)

Row 2 (WS): Sl1, k to mrk, work Pattern A row 2, k2.

Row 3: Sl1, k1, work Pattern A row 3, k to last 2sts, m1, k2. (11sts, with 1st inc'd)

The previous 2 rows set the pattern for the first pattern section.

Continue as set by these 2 rows, working following row of stitch pattern for each subsequent row of swatch pattern as required, until row 10 of Pattern A has been completed. Remove stitch marker while working last row. (14sts after row 10 has been completed)

Explanatory note: There are now enough stitches for an additional repeat of Textured-Triangles Pattern A to be worked. The stitch marker is replaced on the next row. This marker shows where the pattern repeats end on the RS rows and begin on the WS rows. To show that there is more than one repeat of the stitch pattern, a repeat instruction is included in the written pattern for the second pattern section. This instruction can also be used for subsequent repeats.

Second pattern section

Row 1 (RS, placing stitch marker): Sl1, k1, *work Pattern A row 1; rep from * to last 2sts, pm, m1, k2. (15sts, with 1st inc'd)

Row 2 (WS): Sl1, k to mrk, *work Pattern A row 2; rep from * to last 2sts, k2.

Row 3: Sl1, k1, *work Pattern A row 3; rep from * to mrk, k to last 2sts, m1, k2. (16sts, with 1st inc'd)

The previous 2 rows set the pattern for the second pattern section.

Continue as set by these 2 rows, working following row of stitch pattern for each subsequent row of swatch pattern as required, until row 10 of Pattern A has been completed. Remove stitch marker while working last row. (19sts, after row 10 has been completed)

Third pattern section

The previous 10 rows of the second pattern section set the pattern for the rest of the swatch.

Next, work second-pattern-section rows 1–10 once. (24sts after row 10 has been completed)

Explanatory note: Textured-Triangles Pattern B, the garter-stitch textured-triangles pattern, is now introduced for the cast-off border.

Cast-off border

Row 1 (RS, placing stitch marker): Sl1, k1, *work Pattern B row 1; rep from * to last 2sts, pm, m1, k2. (25sts, with 1st inc'd)

Row 2 (WS): Sl1, k to mrk, *work Pattern B row 2; rep from * to last 2sts, k2.

Row 3: Sl1, k1, *work Pattern B row 3; rep from * to mrk, k to last 2sts, m1, k2. (26sts, with 1st inc'd)

Pattern B right-side detail of Textured Triangles swatch.

Pattern B wrong-side detail of Textured Triangles swatch.

The previous 2 rows set the pattern for the cast-off border.

Continue as set by these 2 rows, working following row of stitch pattern for each subsequent row of swatch pattern as required, until row 8 of Pattern B has been completed. Remove stitch marker while working last row. (28sts after row 8 has been completed)

Row 9 (RS): Sl1, k to last 2sts, m1, k2. (29sts, with 1st inc'd)

With WS facing, cast off knitwise.

CHAPTER 7

CIRCLES AND SEMICIRCLES

In the previous three chapters, we have considered a wide variety of straight-sided shapes. The next two chapters consider curved shapes for shawls, beginning with circles and semicircles before moving on to crescent shapes.

A circle is a round shape with all points on its circumference at the same distance from the centre and a semicircle is half of a circle where the circle has been cut along the diameter line. Shawls of these shapes provide opportunities to create beautiful drape and great drama; for example, the wide sweep of a cape-sized circular shawl will have great impact. Circular shapes can be knitted in many different ways, by applying increasing techniques, short-row shaping and mathematical principles.

As with all of the shawl shapes in this book, the starting point is an inspirational source. For this chapter, the inspiration is present in many cities and is often overlooked by passers-by. A rich source of circles and semicircles can be found under our feet as we walk around. In this case,

drain covers inspire the first samples of this chapter. The ornate decorative ironwork patterns can be translated into knitting in many different ways.

Circles and semicircles can inspire a shawl design with symmetrical properties. Many circular designs are radially symmetric, with both rotational and reflective symmetry. Once a single component section is identified, these designs can be surprisingly simple to create. Precisely placing a series of increases can create great movement within a spiral-shawl design,

OPPOSITE: Semicircular drain cover, Brussels, Belgium.

Circular drain cover, Guildford, UK.

drawing the eye from the centre to the outer edges. Using mathematical formulae and concepts such as pi can create shapes that are beautiful to look at and can be enhanced with texture and decoration in many different ways.

Legendary designer Elizabeth Zimmermann had a profound influence on all aspects of knitting. She is the designer who popularized pi shawls and half-pi shawls. Using the mathematical principle of pi, Zimmermann calculated regular increases that occur as the circumference of the circle doubles. She extended the idea to her Pie Are Square composite shawl shape. Most importantly, she encouraged everyone to develop their skills, with many options provided for knitters to customize her patterns. Elizabeth Zimmermann describes the method in the Master Class section (p.112) of her 1984 book *Knitting Workshop*:

> The simplest of all shawls is the Pi Shawl. Governed by Pythagoras' discovery that a circle doubles its circumference in an itself-doubling series of increases, each of which is twice as far apart as the preceding doubled space. Simple, huh? Ask a mathematician.

This chapter considers several methods of knitting circles and semicircles. The placement of the increases particularly impacts the shape and the appearance of the stitch pattern. For example, the circular spiral-

Circle with Spiral Increase Lines – Worked in the Round

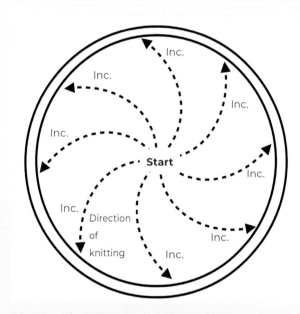

Diagram of a knitted circle with spiral increase lines.

Circle with spiral increase lines swatch, knitted in the round with 3.5mm needles and baa ram ewe Titus 4ply yarn.

Swatch information
Inspiration: Drain cover
Swatch shape: Circle
Increase: M1

Decreases: None
Start: Centre of circle
Centre: Spiral-increase pattern
End: Outer circumference of circle

increase swatch, worked from the centre outwards, has a distinctive effect on the contrast stripe. Each of the increases is worked one stitch position further over than the previous one, moving the lines of increase in a curved spiral pattern. This creates a noticeable jog in the stripe pattern. The outer edges of the circle are also slightly flattened between each of the final increases. With the concentric-increase circle example, the increase lines are placed according to the pi formula. The increased stitches appear in rings, with the space between each ring doubling as the circular swatch grows. These two increase placements both form circles. However, the appearance of the internal stitch pattern is very different.

Both increase placements can also be applied to semicircles with similar effects. However, the construction methods are different, with the semicircles being knitted flat in rows. The semicircular swatches start at the centre of the top edge and therefore also have a top-edge border pattern to be taken into consideration.

Closed increases are used in all four swatches. These vary between m1 and kfb, which have similar appearances in the sample yarn used. The cast-off method used varies between a chain cast-off and a knitted cast-off. The knitted cast-off is looser and can help to provide a neat edge for a curved shape.

Border (outer edge): Garter stitch

Test yarn shown: baa ram ewe Titus 4ply (50-per-cent Wensleydale wool, 20-per-cent Bluefaced Leicester wool, 30-per-cent British alpaca, 320m/350yd per 100g hank)

Yarn A: Shade 008 (Coal); 1 × 100g skein, approximately 10g required for swatch

Yarn B: Shade 002 (Yorkstone); 1 × 100g skein, less than 5g required for swatch

Needles: A set of 3.5mm (UK 9–10/US 4) double-pointed knitting needles

Special abbreviation

kfb: knit front and back – knit into the front and then the back of the next stitch on the left-hand needle, then allow this knitted-into stitch to slip off of the left-hand needle point (1st inc'd).

Swatch instructions

Set-up

Using 3.5mm needles and Yarn A, cast on 8sts by using a loop method (*see* the feature box 'Centre-loop method for a centre start' in Chapter 4).
Place a stitch marker at the start of the round, and join to work in the round.
Knit 1 round.

Round 1 (increase round): Using Yarn A, *k1, m1; rep from * to mrk. (16sts, with 8sts inc'd)

Round 2 and 4 following alternate rounds: Using Yarn A, knit.

Round 3 (increase round): Using Yarn A, *k1, m1, k1; rep from * to mrk. (24sts, with 8sts inc'd)

Round 5 (increase round): Using Yarn A, *k1, m1, k2; rep from * to mrk. (32sts, with 8sts inc'd)

Round 7 (increase round): Using Yarn A, *k1, m1, k3; rep from * to mrk. (40sts, with 8sts inc'd)

Round 9 (increase round): Using Yarn A, *k1, m1, k4; rep from * to mrk. (48sts, with 8sts inc'd)

Contrast stripe

Round 11 (increase round): Using Yarn B, *k1, m1, k5; rep from * to mrk. (56sts, with 8sts inc'd)

Round 12: Using Yarn B, purl.

Outer border

Round 13 (increase round): Using Yarn A, *k1, m1, k6; rep from * to mrk. (64sts, with 8sts inc'd)

Round 14: Using Yarn A, knit.

Round 15 (increase round): Using Yarn A, *k1, m1, k7; rep from * to mrk. (72sts, with 8sts inc'd)

Round 16: Using Yarn A, purl.

Round 17 (increase round): Using Yarn A, *k1, m1, k8; rep from * to mrk. (80sts, with 8sts inc'd)

Round 18: Using Yarn A, cast off purlwise.

Circle with Concentric Increase Lines – Worked in the Round

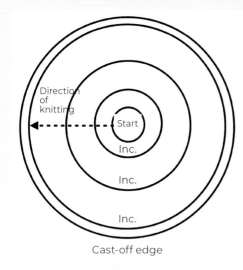

Direction
of
knitting

Start

Inc.

Inc.

Inc.

Cast-off edge

Diagram of a knitted circle with concentric increase lines.

Swatch information

Inspiration: Drain cover
Swatch shape: Circle
Increase: M1
Decreases: None
Start: Centre of circle
Centre: Concentric-increase pattern
End: Outer circumference of circle
Border (outer edge): Garter stitch
Test yarn shown: baa ram ewe Titus 4ply (50-per-cent Wensleydale wool, 20-per-cent Bluefaced Leicester wool, 30-per-cent British alpaca, 320m/350yd per 100g hank)

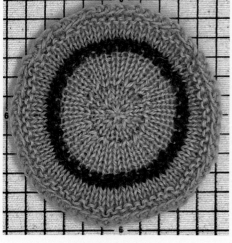

Circle with concentric increase lines swatch, knitted in the round with 3.5mm needles and baa ram ewe Titus 4ply yarn.

Yarn A: Shade 002 (Yorkstone); 1 × 100g skein, approximately 10g required for swatch
Yarn B: Shade 008 (Coal); 1 × 100g skein, less than 5g required for swatch
Needles: A set of 3.5mm (UK 9–10/US 4) double-pointed knitting needles

Swatch instructions

Set-up

Using 3.5mm needles and Yarn A, cast on 4sts by using a loop method (see the feature box 'Centre-loop method for a centre start' in Chapter 4).
Place a stitch marker at the start of the round, and join to work in the round.
Knit 1 round.
Round 1 (increase round): Using Yarn A, *k1, m1; rep from * to mrk. (8sts, with 4sts inc'd)
Round 2: Using Yarn A, knit.
Round 3 (increase round): Using Yarn A, *k1, m1, k1; rep from * to mrk. (16sts, with 8sts inc'd)
Rounds 4–6: Using Yarn A, knit.
Round 7 (increase round): Using Yarn A, work as round 1. (32sts, with 16sts inc'd)
Rounds 8–12: Using Yarn A, knit.

Contrast stripe

Round 13: Using Yarn B, knit.
Round 14: Using Yarn B, purl.

Border

Round 15 (increase round): Using Yarn A, work as row 1. (64sts, with 32sts inc'd)
Rounds 16–19: Using Yarn A, knit.
Round 20: Using Yarn A, purl.
Round 21: Using Yarn A, knit.
To create a loose cast-off edge, cast off as follows:
K2, knit these 2sts together through backs of loops (k2tog-tbl), *k1, knit this stitch together with the stitch already on the right-hand needle (again, k2tog-tbl); rep from * to end.
Fasten off.

Semicircle with Radial Increase Lines – Worked Flat

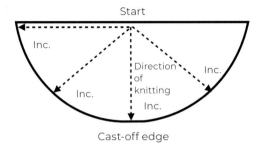

Start

Inc.

Direction of knitting

Inc.

Inc.

Inc.

Cast-off edge

Diagram of a knitted semicircle with radial increase lines.

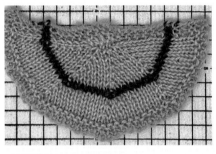

Semicircle with radial increase lines swatch, worked flat, knitted with 3.5mm needles and baa ram ewe Titus 4ply yarn.

Swatch information

Inspiration: Drain cover
Swatch shape: Semicircle
Increase: Kfb
Decreases: None
Start: Garter-stitch tab at centre of top edge
Centre: Radial-increase pattern
End: Outer edge of semicircle
Border (outer edge): Garter stitch
Test yarn shown: baa ram ewe Titus 4ply (50-per-cent Wensleydale wool, 20-per-cent Bluefaced Leicester wool, 30-per-cent British alpaca, 320m/350yd per 100g hank)
Yarn A: Shade 002 (Yorkstone); 1 × 100g skein, approximately 10g required for swatch
Yarn B: Shade 008 (Coal); 1 × 100g skein, less than 5g required for swatch
Needles: A pair 3.5mm (UK 9–10/US 4) knitting needles

Swatch instructions

Set-up
Using 3.5mm needles and Yarn A, cast on 3sts. Knit 9 rows. After working the ninth row (RS), do not turn work.

Next, with 3sts on right-hand needle, pick up and knit 4sts along side of tab and 3sts along cast-on edge. (10sts)
Next row (WS): Using Yarn A, sl1, k1, p to last 2sts, k2.

Increase section
Row 1 (RS, increase row): Using Yarn A, sl1, k2, *kfb; rep from * to last 3sts, k3. (14sts, with 4sts inc'd)
Row 2 and 4 following WS rows: Using Yarn A, sl1, k2, p to last 3sts, k3.
Row 3 (increase row): Using Yarn A, sl1, k2, *kfb, k1; rep from * to last 3sts, k3. (18sts, with 4sts inc'd)
Row 5 (increase row): Using Yarn A, sl1, k2, *kfb, k2; rep from * to last 3sts, k3. (22sts, with 4sts inc'd)
Row 7 (increase row): Using Yarn A, sl1, k2, *kfb, k3; rep from * to last 3sts, k3. (26sts, with 4sts inc'd)
Row 9 (increase row): Using Yarn A, sl1, k2, *kfb, k4; rep from * to last 3sts, k3. (30sts, with 4sts inc'd)

Contrast-stripe section
Row 11 (increase row): Using Yarn B, *sl1, k2, *kfb, k5; rep from * to last 3sts, k3. (34sts, with 4sts inc'd)
Row 12: Using Yarn B, sl1, k to end.
Row 13 (increase row): Using Yarn A, *sl1, k2, *kfb, k6; rep from * to last 3sts, k3. (38sts, with 4sts inc'd)
Row 14 and 2 following WS rows: Using Yarn A, sl1, k2, p to last 3sts, k3.
Row 15 (increase row): Using Yarn A, *sl1, k2, *kfb, k7; rep from * to last 3sts, k3. (42sts, with 4sts inc'd)
Row 17 (increase row): Using Yarn A, *sl1, k2, *kfb, k8; rep from * to last 3sts, k3. (46sts, with 4sts inc'd)
Row 19 (increase row): Using Yarn A, *sl1, k2, *kfb, k9; rep from * to last 3sts, k3. (50sts, with 4sts inc'd)

Border
Row 20: Using Yarn A, work as row 12.
Row 21 (increase row): Using Yarn A, *sl1, k2, *kfb, k10; rep from * to last 3sts, k3. (54sts, with 4sts inc'd)
Using Yarn A, cast off loosely as follows: K2, knit these 2sts together through backs of loops (k2tog-tbl), *k1, knit this stitch together with the stitch already on the right-hand needle (again, k2tog-tbl); rep from * to end. Fasten off.

Semicircle with Concentric Increase Lines – Worked Flat

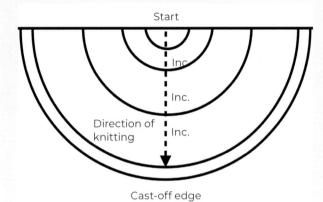

Diagram of a knitted semicircle with concentric increases.

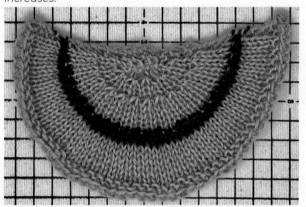

Semicircle with concentric increase lines swatch, worked flat, knitted with 3.5mm needles and baa ram ewe Titus 4ply yarn.

Swatch information

Inspiration: Drain cover
Swatch shape: Semicircle
Increase: Kfb
Decreases: None
Start: Garter-stitch tab at centre of top edge
Centre: Concentric-increase pattern
End: Outer edge of semicircle
Border (outer edge): Garter stitch
Test yarn shown: baa ram ewe Titus 4ply
(50-per-cent Wensleydale wool, 20-per-cent

Bluefaced Leicester wool, 30-per-cent British alpaca, 320m/350yd per 100g hank)
Yarn A: Shade 002 (Yorkstone); 1 × 100g skein, approximately 10g required for swatch
Yarn B: Shade 008 (Coal); 1 × 100g skein, less than 5g required for swatch
Needles: A pair 3.5mm (UK 9–10/US 4) knitting needles

Swatch instructions

Set-up

Using 3.5mm needles and Yarn A, cast on 3sts.
Knit 9 rows. After working the ninth row (RS), do not turn work.
Next, with 3sts on right-hand needle, pick up and knit 4sts along side of tab and 3sts along cast-on edge. (10sts)
Next row (WS): Using Yarn A, *sl1, k1, p to last 2sts, k2.

Increase section

Row 1 (RS, increase row): Using Yarn A, sl1, k1, *kfb; rep from * to last 2sts, k2. (16sts, with 6sts inc'd)
Row 2 (WS): Using Yarn A, sl1, k1, p to last 2sts, k2.
Row 3: Using Yarn A, sl1, k to end.
Row 4: Using Yarn A, work as row 2.
Row 5 (increase row): Using Yarn A, work as row 1. (28sts, with 12sts inc'd)
Rows 6–10: Using Yarn A, work as rows 2–3, ending with a WS row 2.

Contrast stripe

Row 11 (increase row): Using Yarn B, work as row 1. (52sts, with 24sts inc'd)
Row 12: Using Yarn B, work as row 3.

Border

Rows 13–19: Using Yarn A, work as rows 2–3, beginning and ending with a RS row 3.
Row 20: Using Yarn A, work as row 3.
Using Yarn A, cast off loosely as follows: K2, knit these 2sts together through backs of loops (k2tog-tbl), *k1, knit this stitch together with the stitch already on the right-hand needle (k2tog-tbl); rep from * to end. Fasten off.

Semicircle with Short-Row Construction

The inspiration for a different construction method is a spiral staircase on the Barbican Estate in London, UK. The metal stairs are arranged around a central supporting pole and, when viewed from above, take on the appearance of a semicircle. The yellow safety-marking painted edges of each step are represented in the swatch as garter-stitch ridges.

In contrast to the last two examples, this next method uses wedges of short rows to build up the sections of a semicircle. There are eight wedges, each divided by a garter-ridge stripe worked in the contrast shade. The contrast yarn is carried along the edge of the work and twisted together with the main shade at the beginning of each row. However, remember not to pull the yarn too tight, and allow the wedges to spread out fully.

Spiral staircase, Barbican Estate, London, UK.

Semicircle with Short-Row Construction – Worked Flat

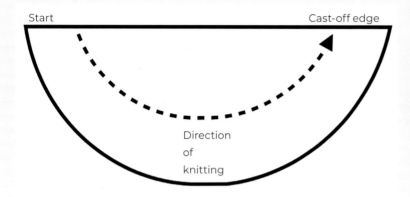

Diagram of semicircle knitted with short-row shaping.

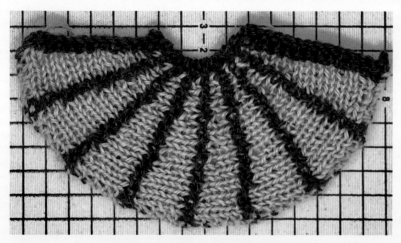

Semicircle with short row shaping swatch, worked flat, knitted with 3.5mm needles and baa ram ewe Titus 4ply yarn.

Swatch information

Inspiration: Spiral staircase, Barbican Estate, London, UK

Swatch shape: Semicircle

Increases: None

Decreases: None

Start: Cast-on edge

Centre: Short-row-shaping pattern

End: Cast-off edge

Border (outer edge): Garter stitch

Test yarn shown: baa ram ewe Titus 4ply (50-per-cent Wensleydale wool, 20-per-cent Bluefaced Leicester wool, 30-per-cent British alpaca, 320m/350yd per 100g hank)

Yarn A: Shade 002 (Yorkstone); 1 × 100g skein, approximately 10g required for swatch

Yarn B: Shade 008 (Coal); 1 × 100g skein, approximately 10g required for swatch

Needles: A pair 3.5mm (UK 9–10/US 4) knitting needles

Special instruction

Short-row (SR) shaping: Short-row shaping is used within each segment of the shape. A stitch is wrapped to avoid a gap remaining in the knitting where each short row is worked. This wrapping action is known as wrap and turn, 'w&t'. For this pattern, to wrap a stitch, knit to the stitch to be wrapped; slip the next stitch purlwise; take the yarn to the back of the work; slip the slipped stitch back to the left-hand needle purlwise without working it; take the yarn to the front of the work; and turn the work. When the wrapped stitch is reached on the subsequent row, work the wrap loop and the wrapped stitch together to close the gap between the wrapped stitch and the adjacent stitch.

Swatch instructions

Set-up
Using 3.5mm needles and Yarn B, cast on 15sts.

Row 1 (RS): Using Yarn B, sl1, k to end.

Row 2 (WS): Using Yarn B, work as row 1.

Main swatch section
Row 3: Work SRs within this row as follows:

SR1 (RS): Using Yarn A, k3, w&t;

SR2 and all following WS SRs: Using Yarn A, p to last 2sts, k2.

SR3: Using Yarn A, sl1, k6, w&t;

SR5: Using Yarn A, sl1, k9, w&t;

SR7: Using Yarn A, sl1, k12, w&t;

SR9: Using Yarn B, sl1, k to end.

Row 4: Using Yarn B, work as row 1.

The previous 4 rows, including SRs1–9, set the pattern.

Work these rows another seven times.

Cast-off border
Using Yarn B, with RS facing, work as row 1.

Using Yarn B, cast off knitwise.

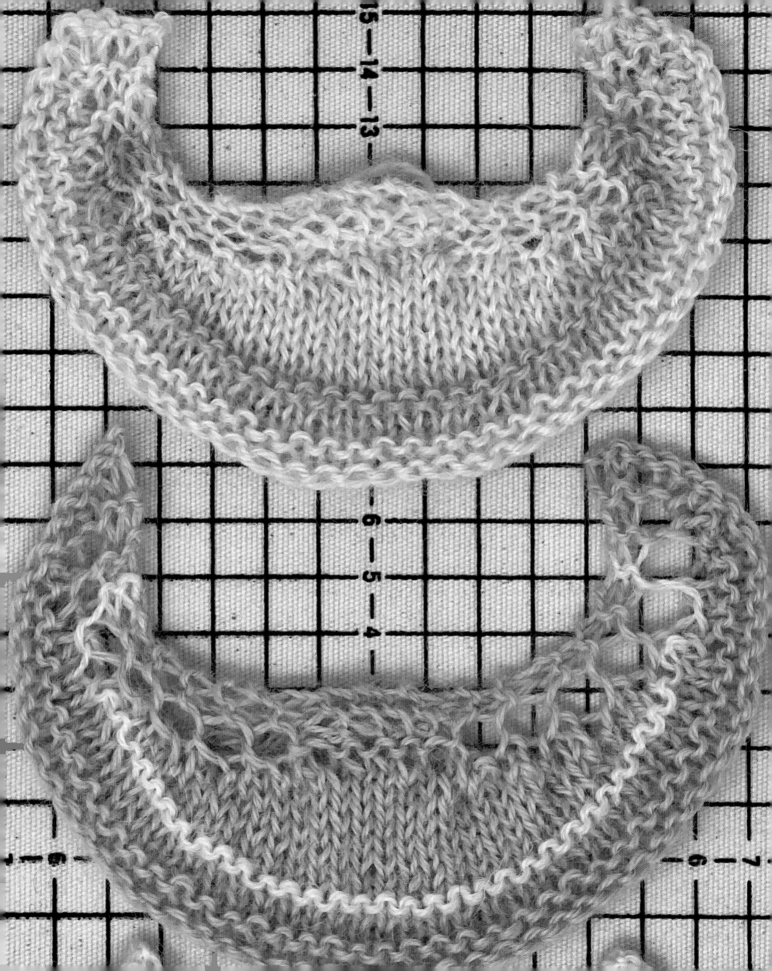

CHAPTER 8

CRESCENTS

A crescent is a curved shape that is usually wider in the middle than at its ends. Whether deep and wide or narrow and long, crescent shawls drape naturally around the shoulders. Depending on the construction method used, crescents can have a series of straight edges that can be blocked into smooth curves.

This chapter begins by considering three main methods to knit a crescent shape: point-to-point, top-down and short-row shaping. The three methods provide many opportunities to customize the construction by using a wide range of different increase methods. The direction of knitting of each method is also an important factor when considering the placement of pattern.

The point-to-point method is similar to shaping explored for the right-angled-triangle sections. The top-down-constructed crescents begin in a similar way to a top-down triangle. However, working additional increases at the top edge creates a curve, rather than a straight edge. Using short-row shaping to create a crescent is an excellent way to create a wide, elongated shape. This method can be worked from the top of the shape downwards or from the bottom upwards.

OPPOSITE: Crescent swatches worked with different top-down construction methods.

Crescent-shaped water sculpture, Tiburon, California, USA.

Information Common to All Swatches in this Section

Inspiration: Crescent-shaped water sculpture, Tiburon, California, USA
Swatch shape: Crescent
Test yarn shown: baa ram ewe Titus 4ply (50-per-cent Wensleydale wool, 20-per-cent Bluefaced Leicester wool, 30-per-cent British alpaca, 320m/350yd per 100g hank)
Yarn A: See individual swatch instructions
Yarn B: See individual swatch instructions
Needles: A pair 3.5mm (UK 9–10/US 4) knitting needles

The inspiration for the crescent shapes in this section is the beautiful curve of a crescent-shaped water feature in Tiburon, California, USA. This water feature has several properties that are fascinating. When viewed when you are standing next to the base, the reflection in the water gives the appearance of a full crescent shape. As the central blade structure rotates, sections of the shape become more or less prominent, changing the depth of the overall shape. Depending on the time of day, the angle of the sunlight reflected on to the water alters, creating a dappled effect. This ever-changing sculpture is the perfect starting point to explore several crescent shapes and their properties.

Crescent Worked Point to Point

This crescent shape is knitted from point to point, creating a shape that is similar to an elongated triangle. This shape consists of two right-angled triangles that meet at their short straight edges. Additional rows are worked between the two triangular sections.

The first point of this crescent shape is knitted in the same way as for a right-angled triangle. The shape is then increased in size to the desired width. At this stage, extra rows are worked to extend the centre of the shape, the crescent, which is then decreased to the second point. This second triangular section matches the first triangular section. Extra curvature can be added to the shape during the finishing process. The

edges can be pinned and deeper curves created, forming a more distinctive crescent shape.

The increases chosen can be open or closed, depending on the final stitch pattern. A horizontally knitted line of pattern appears vertical when a shape knitted by using this method is draped around the shoulders. The placement of pattern can divide the shawl into sections. As can be seen in the accompanying swatch image, the horizontally knitted stripe cuts the shape in half.

Crescent Worked Top Down

The top-down crescent shape begins with a garter-stitch tab. From this tab, the shawl is knitted downwards with multiple increases being worked at the top edge. There are several different options for the placement of these increases, and this section explores three. The accompanying image demonstrates these three different placements of the increases. The top two swatches have increases worked over two rows, and, for the bottom swatch, the increases are worked on right-side rows only. There are mainly subtle differences between the swatches. The choice of increases will depend on the main stitch pattern and the particular characteristics of the yarn being used.

The first swatch includes two different types of closed increases. The first type is used on right-side rows and creates two new stitches by working three times into

Crescent Worked Point to Point

Swatch information

Increases: (K1, p1, k1) all into next st, m1
Decrease: Ssk
Start: Point of crescent
Centre: Increase to full width, work straight, decrease to point
End: Point of crescent
Borders (straight and curved edges): Garter stitch
Yarn A: Shade 002 (Yorkstone); 1 × 100g skein, approximately 10g required for swatch
Yarn B: Shade 021 (Brass Band); 1 × 100g skein, less than 5g required for swatch

Special abbreviation

kfb: knit front and back – knit into the front and then the back of the next stitch on the left-hand needle, then allow this knitted-into stitch to slip off of the left-hand needle point (1st inc'd).

Swatch instructions

Lower point

Using 3.5mm needles and Yarn A, cast on 1st.
Row 1 (RS): Using Yarn A, k1, p1, k1 all into same st. (3sts, with 2sts inc'd)
Row 2 (WS): Using Yarn A, knit.
Row 3: Using Yarn A, k1, (k1, p1, k1) all into next st, k1. (5sts, with 2sts inc'd)
Row 4: Using Yarn A, sl1, k to end.

Increase section

Row 1 (RS): Using Yarn A, sl1, k to last 2sts, m1, k2. (6sts, with 1st inc'd)
Row 2 (WS): Using Yarn A, sl1, k1, p to last 2sts, k2.
Row 3: Using Yarn A, sl1, k to end.
Row 4: Using Yarn A, work as row 2.
The previous 4 rows set the increase pattern.
Next, work these 4 rows another eight times. (14sts, after final row 4 has been completed)
Next, work rows 3–4 once more.

Contrast-stripe section

Row 1 (RS): Using Yarn B, sl1, k to end.
Row 2 (WS): Using Yarn B, work as row 1.

Rows 3–6: Using Yarn A, work as increase-section rows 3–4.

Decrease section

Row 1 (RS): Using Yarn A, sl1, k to last 3sts, ssk, k1. (13sts, with 1st dec'd)
Rows 2 and 4 (WS): Using Yarn A, work as increase-section row 2.
Row 3: Using Yarn A, work as increase-section row 3.
The previous 4 rows set the decrease pattern.
Next, work these 4 rows another six times. (7sts, after final row 4 has been completed)

Upper point

Row 1 (RS): Using Yarn A, sl1, k1, sl1, k2tog, psso, k2. (5sts, with 2sts dec'd)
Row 2 (WS): Using Yarn A, sl1, k to end.
Row 3 (RS): Using Yarn A, k1, sl1, k2tog, psso, k1. (3sts, with 2sts dec'd)
Row 4: Using Yarn A, knit.
Row 5: Using Yarn A, sl1, k2tog, psso. (1st, with 2sts dec'd)
Fasten off.

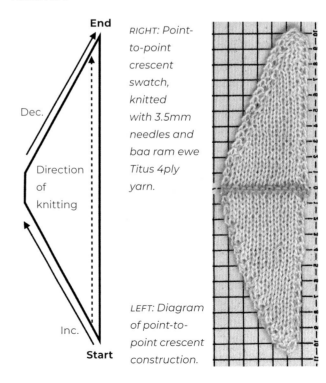

RIGHT: Point-to-point crescent swatch, knitted with 3.5mm needles and baa ram ewe Titus 4ply yarn.

LEFT: Diagram of point-to-point crescent construction.

Crescent Worked Top Down – Closed Increases Over Two Rows

Swatch information

Increases: (K1, p1, k1) all into next st on RS rows, kfb on WS rows

Decreases: None

Start: Garter-stitch tab

Centre: Increase pattern

End: Cast-off edge

Borders (top and outer edge): Garter stitch

Yarn A: Shade 002 (Yorkstone); 1 × 100g skein, approximately 10g required for swatch

Yarn B: Shade 021 (Brass Band); 1 × 100g skein, less than 5g required for swatch

Swatch instructions

Set-up

Using 3.5mm needles and Yarn A, cast on 3sts.

Knit 9 rows. After working the ninth row (RS), do not turn work.

Next, with 3sts on right-hand needle, pick up and knit 4sts along side of tab and 3sts along cast-on edge. (10sts)

Next row (WS): Using Yarn A, sl1, k to end.

Increase section

Row 1 (RS): Using Yarn A, sl1, k1, (k1, p1, k1) all into next st, k to last 3sts, (k1, p1, k1) all into next stitch, k2. (14sts, with 4sts inc'd)

Row 2 (WS): Using Yarn A, sl1, k2, kfb, p to last 4sts, kfb, k3. (16sts, with 2sts inc'd)

The previous 2 rows set the increase pattern.

Rows 3–8: Using Yarn A, work as rows 1–2. (34sts, after row 8 has been completed)

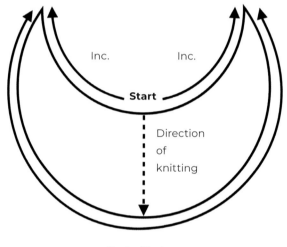

Diagram of top-down crescent construction.

Crescent Worked Top Down – Open Increases Over Two Rows

Swatch information

Increases: Yo, k1, yo on RS rows, yo on WS rows

Decreases: None

Start: Garter-stitch tab

Centre: Increase pattern

End: Cast-off edge

Borders (top and outer edge): Garter stitch

Yarn A: Shade 021 (Brass Band); 1 × 100g skein, approximately 10g required for swatch

Yarn B: Shade 002 (Yorkstone); 1 × 100g skein, less than 5g required for swatch

Swatch instructions

Set-up

Using 3.5mm needles and Yarn A, cast on 3sts.

Knit 9 rows. After working the ninth row (RS), do not turn work.

Next, with 3sts on right-hand needle, pick up and knit 4sts along side of tab and 3sts along cast-on edge. (10sts)

Next row (WS): Using Yarn A, sl1, k to end.

Contrast-stripe section

Row 9: Using Yarn B, work as row 1. (38sts, with 4sts inc'd)

Row 10: Using Yarn B, sl1, k2, kfb, k to last 4sts, kfb, k3. (40sts, with 2sts inc'd)

Rows 11–13: Using Yarn A, work as rows 1–2, ending with a RS row 1. (50sts, after row 13 has been completed)

Cast-off border

Row 14: Using Yarn A, work as row 10. (52sts, with 2sts inc'd)

Row 15: Using Yarn A, work as row 1. (56sts, with 4sts inc'd)

Using Yarn A, cast off knitwise.

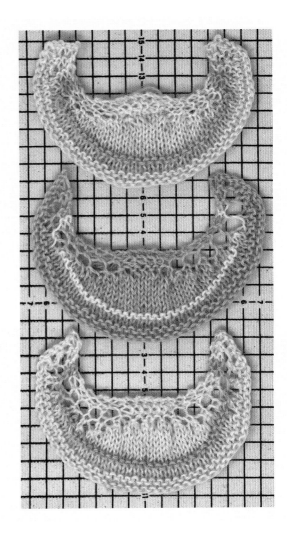

Top-down construction crescent swatches, knitted with 3.5mm needles and baa ram ewe Titus 4ply yarn. Top swatch: closed increases worked over two rows; middle swatch: open increases worked over two rows; bottom swatch: open increases worked on right-side rows only.

Increase section

Row 1 (RS): Using Yarn A, sl1, k1, yo, k1, yo, k to last 3sts, yo, k1, yo, k2. (14sts, with 4sts inc'd)

Row 2 (WS): Using Yarn A, sl1, k2, yo, p to last 4sts, yo, k3. (16sts, with 2sts inc'd)

The previous 2 rows set the increase pattern.

Rows 3–8: Using Yarn A, work as for rows 1–2. (34sts, after row 8 has been completed)

Contrast-stripe section

Row 9: Using Yarn B, work as row 1. (38sts, with 4sts inc'd)

Row 10: Using Yarn B, sl1, k2, yo, k to last 4sts, yo, k3. (40sts, with 2sts inc'd)

Rows 11–13: Using Yarn A, work as rows 1–2, ending with a RS row 1. (50sts, after row 13 has been completed)

Cast-off border

Row 14: Using Yarn A, work as row 10. (52sts, with 2sts inc'd)

Row 15: Using Yarn A, work as row 1. (56sts, with 4sts inc'd)

Using Yarn A, cast off knitwise.

one stitch. The second type creates one new stitch by working twice into the same stitch. By working these two types of increase over two rows, the increases are spread out, helping to maintain elasticity along the increased edge of the shawl shape. Elasticity is one of the most important factors for a crescent shawl and can be hard to maintain. It is vital to test the preferred increase pattern in the particular yarn to be used.

The increases used for the second swatch are also worked over two rows. This time, an open increase is used. There is considerably more elasticity along the top edge of this swatch compared to that the first swatch with closed increases. The eyelets form a decorative border along the edge.

The third swatch shape is formed with yarn overs worked on right-side rows only. This approach forms a decorative eyelet border and has good elasticity along the top edge of the shape.

These three swatches demonstrate that there are many different combinations of increase patterns to choose from. A balance between the factors of decoration and elasticity is achieved through trial and error of using each method.

In all three swatches, the placement of a horizontally knitted line of pattern appears as a crescent curve. As this contrast stripe is worked close to the outer edge of the shape, in this case, it closely matches the curve of the outer edge.

Crescent Worked With Short-Row Shaping

Two very similar crescent shapes can be knitted by using short-row shaping techniques. Although their

Crescent Worked Top Down – Open Increases Over Right-Side Rows Only

Swatch information
Increase: Yo, (k1, yo) twice on RS rows only
Decreases: None
Start: Garter-stitch tab
Centre: Increase pattern
End: Cast-off edge
Borders (top and outer edge): Garter stitch
Yarn A: Shade 002 (Yorkstone); 1 × 100g skein, approximately 10g required for swatch
Yarn B: Shade 021 (Brass Band); 1 × 100g skein, less than 5g required for swatch

Swatch instructions
Set-up
Using 3.5mm needles and Yarn A, cast on 3sts.
Knit 9 rows. After working the ninth row (RS), do not turn work.
Next, with 3sts on right-hand needle, pick up and knit 4sts along side of tab and 3sts along cast-on edge. (10sts)
Next row (WS): Using Yarn A, sl1, k to end.

Increase section
Row 1 (RS): Using Yarn A, sl1, k1, yo, (k1, yo) twice, k to last 4sts, (yo, k1) twice, yo, k2. (16sts, with 6sts inc'd)
Row 2 (WS): Using Yarn A, sl1, k1, p to last 2sts, k2.
The previous 2 rows set the increase pattern.
Rows 3–8: Using Yarn A, work as rows 1–2 rows. (34sts, after row 8 has been completed)

Contrast-stripe section
Row 9: Using Yarn B, work as row 1. (40sts, with 6sts inc'd)
Row 10: Using Yarn B, sl1, k to end.
Rows 11–13: Using Yarn A, work as rows 1–2, ending with a RS row 1. (50sts, after row 13 has been completed)

Cast-off border
Row 14: Using Yarn A, work as row 10.
Row 15: Using Yarn A, work as row 1. (56sts, with 6sts inc'd)
Using Yarn A, cast off knitwise.

initial appearance is similar, these shapes start differently, and this has implications for the chosen stitch-pattern placement.

The top-down construction method builds the curve by working from the top of the shape towards the bottom. Stitches are cast on for the full width of the shape. The longest short rows are worked first across almost the full width of the shawl, building the curve from the top downwards. A wide, shallow crescent shape can be formed by using this method. This makes it ideal for the top of a shawl that continues with a different stitch pattern in the lower section.

The bottom-up construction method begins with the shortest short rows being worked first in the centre of the lower edge of the shape. The curve is built up from the bottom of the shape towards the top. This method is particularly useful for shawls that require the crescent shaping at the lower, wide edge. Another shape, such as a wide rectangle, can be worked at the top of the crescent, creating the possibility of adding a contrasting back-of-neck and shoulder section.

Special Instruction for Crescents Worked with Short-Row Shaping

Short-row (SR) shaping: Short-row shaping is used to create the crescent shape. A stitch is wrapped to avoid a gap remaining in the knitting where each short row is worked. This wrapping action is known as wrap and turn, 'w&t'. For this pattern, to wrap a stitch, knit to the stitch to be wrapped; slip the next stitch purlwise; take the yarn to the back of the work; slip the slipped stitch back to the left-hand needle purlwise without working it; take the yarn to the front of the work; and turn the work. When the wrapped stitches are reached on the final row, work the wrap loops and the wrapped stitches together to close the gaps between the wrapped stitch and the adjacent stitch.

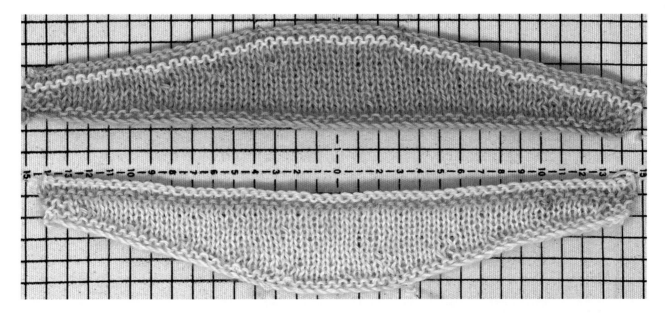

Short-row crescent swatches, knitted with 3.5mm needles and baa ram ewe Titus 4ply yarn: top down (yellow with white stripe) and bottom up (white with yellow stripe).

Crescent Worked Top Down with Short-Row Shaping

Swatch information

Increases: None

Decreases: None

Start: Top cast-on edge

Centre: Short-row-shaping pattern

End: Bottom cast-off edge

Borders (top, side and bottom edges): Garter stitch

Yarn A: Shade 021 (Brass Band); 1 × 100g skein, approximately 10g required for swatch

Yarn B: Shade 002 (Yorkstone); 1 × 100g skein, less than 5g required for swatch

Swatch instructions

Set-up

Using 3.5mm needles and Yarn A, cast on 58sts.

Row 1 (RS): Using Yarn A, sl1, k to end.

Row 2 (WS): Using Yarn A, work as row 1.

Main swatch section

Row 1 (RS): Using Yarn A, work SRs within this row as follows:

SR1 (RS): K55, w&t;

SR2 (WS): P52, w&t;

SR3: K47, w&t;

SR4: P42, w&t;

SR5: K37, w&t;

SR6: P32, w&t;

SR7: K27, w&t;

SR8: P22, w&t;

SR9: K17, w&t;

SR10: P12, w&t;

SR11: K to end.

Row 2 (WS): Using Yarn A, sl1, k2, p to last 3sts, k3.

Contrast stripe

Row 1 (RS): Using Yarn B, sl1, k to end.

Row 2 (WS): Using Yarn B, work as row 1.

Cast-off border

Row 3: Using Yarn A, work as row 1.

Using Yarn A, cast off knitwise.

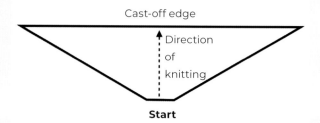

Diagram of top-down crescent with short-row construction.

Crescent Worked Bottom Up with Short-Row Shaping

Swatch information

Increases: None

Decreases: None

Start: Bottom cast-on edge

Centre: Short-row-shaping pattern

End: Top cast-off edge

Borders (top, side and bottom edges): Garter stitch

Yarn A: Shade 002 (Yorkstone); 1 × 100g skein, approximately 10g required for swatch

Yarn B: Shade 021 (Brass Band); 1 × 100g skein, less than 5g required for swatch

Swatch instructions

Set-up

Using 3.5mm needles and Yarn A, cast on 58sts.

Row 1 (RS): Using Yarn A, sl1, k to end.

Row 2 (WS): Using Yarn A, work as row 1.

Main swatch section

Row 1 (RS): Using Yarn A, work SRs within this row as follows:

SR1 (RS): K34, w&t;

SR2 (WS): P10, w&t;

SR3: K15, w&t;

SR4: P20, w&t;

SR5: K25, w&t;

SR6: P30, w&t;

SR7: K35, w&t;

SR8: P40, w&t;

SR9: K45, w&t;

SR10: P50, w&t;

SR11: K to end.

Row 2 (WS): Using Yarn A, sl1, k2, p to last 3sts, k3.

Contrast stripe

Row 1 (RS): Using Yarn B, sl1, k to end.

Row 2 (WS): Using Yarn B, work as row 1.

Cast-off border

Row 3: Using Yarn A, work as row 1.

Using Yarn A, cast off knitwise.

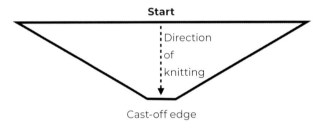

Diagram of bottom-up crescent with short-row construction.

Part 3
SHAWL PATTERNS

INTRODUCTION

The final part of this book places all of the previous design development into context within a series of shawl patterns. These patterns can be knitted straight away in their current form or be used to inspire new designs. Each shawl pattern includes stitch patterns that can also be used in other projects, as desired.

Although the patterns are very different from each other, they all have a similar design-development process. Each design begins with researching or visiting an inspirational source, before considering shape and pattern possibilities. Following the initial design steps, decisions about yarn fibre and colour can be made. By working from the inspirational source in this way, many opportunities for customization are created.

I encourage you to explore and experiment whenever possible and, most of all, to enjoy discovering new pattern possibilities through your own knitting designs!

OPPOSITE: The crescent shape of the Modernism Shawl consists of two triangles separated by a rectangle. (Photographed by Maxine Vining.)

CHAPTER 9

RIVERSIDE SHAWL

Design Details

Inspiration

Home to over three-thousand items relating to transport in the city of Glasgow, the Riverside Museum of Transport has objects ranging from cars, motorbikes and buses to posters and model ships. The building was designed by Zaha Hadid Architects and opened in June 2011. Its front and back facades have dramatic zigzag rooflines and vast glass frontages. These distinctive peaks and troughs were the perfect inspiration for the Riverside Shawl's chevron patterns. The shawl is knitted in three parts: a central panel and two outer wings.

Shape

The overall shape of this shawl is best described as an extended rectangle, comprising one square and two rectangles. The central-square panel is knitted first, worked from edge to edge, then the two outer-rectangle wings are worked, one at a time, by stitches being picked up and knitted outwards from one of the sides of the square. These outer-rectangle wings have been altered to form a trapezium. For the Riverside Shawl, the trapezium shape has four straight sides with one set of opposite sides being parallel, and the wings are wider at the outer cast-off edges.

ABOVE AND RIGHT: Two views of the Riverside Museum, Glasgow, UK.

Roof detail of the Riverside Museum, Glasgow, UK.

All three of these shapes have been extended and altered by the addition of the chevron stitch pattern to form dramatic zigzags. The outer side edges of the central square remain as straight edges. A further enhancement is made by working the first and last rows in the contrast shade of yarn, drawing attention to the chevron points and recesses. This reversed colourway for the outer sections is also a practical way to ensure effective use of each yarn-shade quantity within the design.

Design development

Taking inspiration directly from the museum roofline, the cast-on and cast-off edges of the square, and the cast-off edges of the rectangles, are worked in a zigzag chevron pattern. Further zigzag chevrons in each shawl section are altered as they are knitted: wide zigzag sections narrow and narrow zigzag sections expand.

Yarn and swatching

The colours selected are linked to the subtle shades of grey that are present in the building on an overcast day. The contrast shade represents the bright green that is used extensively in the museum's interior. Using strong contrast enhances the optical effect of the different chevron patterns.

The test swatch, worked in a variation of the main-shawl stitch pattern, has a single increasing chevron and a single decreasing chevron. This small swatch demonstrates how increasing and decreasing within the stitch pattern can be used to change the widths of the two chevron sections at the same time, while maintaining the same overall number of stitches.

The full shawl pattern extends this idea by the chevrons being worked over more stitches and rows. Other modifications used in the full shawl pattern include increasing the width of the reverse-stocking-stitch stripes, working additional decreases at the cast-off edge, to emphasize the chevron points, and maintaining the straight sides of the central-square shape, by working a balanced set of chevron increases and decreases.

Swatch Information

Riverside swatch, knitted with 3.5mm needles and John Arbon Knit By Numbers 4ply yarn.

Inspiration: Riverside Museum of Transport, Glasgow, UK
Shape: Rectangle
Increase: Yo
Decreases: K2tog, sk2po, ssk
Start: Cast-on edge of rectangle
End: Cast-off border of rectangle
Border (side edges): Garter stitch
Border (cast-on and -off edges): Reverse-stocking-stitch ridges

Test yarn shown: John Arbon Knit By Numbers (KBN) 4ply (100-per-cent pure Falklands merino wool, 400m/437yd per 100g skein)
Yarn A: Shade KBN05 (mid-grey); 1 × 100g skein, approximately 20g required for swatch
Yarn B: Shade KBN71 (green); 1 × 100g skein, approximately 10g required for swatch
Needles: A pair 3.5mm (UK 9–10/US 4) knitting needles

Swatch Instructions (Two Chevrons, Worked Over Six Sections)

Use two contrasting shades of yarn of choice with appropriate needle size.

Set-up
Using Yarn A, cast on 23sts.
Knit 2 rows, slipping the first stitch of each row.

Section 1
Row 1 (RS): Using Yarn A, sl1, k1, yo, sk2po, yo, k1, yo, k6, sk2po, k6, yo, k2.
Row 2 (WS): Using Yarn A, sl1, k1, p to last 2sts, k2.
Rows 3–4: Using Yarn A, work as rows 1–2.
Row 5 (increase and decrease row): Using Yarn B, sl1, k1, yo, k3, yo, k1, yo, k4, k2tog, sk2po, ssk, k4, yo, k2.
Row 6: Using Yarn B, sl1, k to end.

Section 2
Row 1 (RS): Using Yarn A, sl1, k1, yo, k1, sk2po, k1, yo, k1, yo, k5, sk2po, k5, yo, k2.
Rows 2 and 4 (WS): Using Yarn A, work as Section 1 row 2.
Row 3: Using Yarn A, work as row 1.
Row 5 (increase and decrease row): Using Yarn B, sl1, k1, yo, k5, yo, k1, yo, k3, k2tog, sk2po, ssk, k3, yo, k2.
Row 6: Using Yarn B, work as Section 1 row 6.

Section 3
Row 1 (RS): Using Yarn A, sl1, k1, yo, k2, sk2po, k2, yo, k1, yo, k4, sk2po, k4, yo, k2.
Rows 2 and 4: Using Yarn A, work as Section 1 row 2.
Row 3: Using Yarn A, work as row 1.
Row 5 (increase and decrease row): Using Yarn B, sl1, k1, yo, k7, yo, k1, yo, k2, k2tog, sk2po, ssk, k2, yo, k2.
Row 6: Using Yarn B, work as Section 1 row 6.

Section 4
Row 1 (RS): Using Yarn A, sl1, k1, yo, k3, sk2po, k3, yo, k1, yo, k3, sk2po, k3, yo, k2.
Rows 2 and 4: Using Yarn A, work as Section 1 row 2.
Row 3: Using Yarn A, work as row 1.
Row 5 (increase and decrease row): Using Yarn B, sl1, k1, yo, k9, yo, k1, yo, k1, k2tog, sk2po, ssk, k1, yo, k2.
Row 6: Using Yarn B, work as Section 1 row 6.

Section 5
Row 1 (RS): Using Yarn A, sl1, k1, yo, k4, sk2po, k4, yo, k1, yo, k2, sk2po, k2, yo, k2.
Rows 2 and 4: Using Yarn A, work as Section 1 row 2.
Row 3: Using Yarn A, work as row 1.
Row 5 (increase and decrease row): Using Yarn B, sl1, k1, yo, k11, yo, k1, yo, k2tog, sk2po, ssk, yo, k2.
Row 6: Using Yarn B, work as Section 1 row 6.

Section 6
Row 1 (RS): Using Yarn A, sl1, k1, yo, k5, sk2po, k5, yo, k1, yo, k1, sk2po, k1, yo, k2.
Rows 2 and 4: Using Yarn A, work as Section 1 row 2.
Row 3: Using Yarn A, work as row 1.
Row 5 (increase and decrease row): Using Yarn B, sl1, k1, yo, k13, yo, k1, yo, sl2, k3tog, pass 2 slipped sts over, yo, k2.
Row 6: Using Yarn B, cast off knitwise.
Block swatch according to instructions on yarn ball band.

Riverside Shawl Pattern

The Riverside Shawl.

Size

Whole shawl
31cm/12in (centre-square depth); 40cm/15¾in (rectangle cast-off width); 131cm/51½in (length)

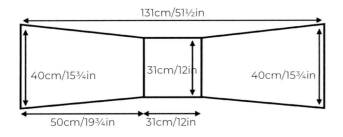

Blocking diagram for the Riverside Shawl.

The back of the Riverside Shawl, showing the centre-square section.

Centre square
31cm/12in (width); 31cm/12in (chevron indent-to-indent depth); 35cm/14in (chevron point-to-point depth)

Rectangle wings (both alike)
31cm/12in (starting width); 40cm/15¾in (cast-off width); 50cm/19¾in (length)

Yarns

John Arbon Knit By Numbers (KBN) 4ply (100-per-cent pure Falklands merino wool, 400m/437yd per 100g skein)

Yarn A: KBN71 (green); 1 × 100g skein
Yarn B: KBN03 (dark grey); 1 × 100g skein
Yarn amounts given are based on average requirements and are approximate.

Accessories

A pair 3.5mm (UK 9–10/US 4) knitting needles

Tensions

28sts × 40 rows to 10cm/4in × 10cm/4in over chevron pattern (*see* Centre Square and Rectangle Wings), using 3.5mm needles
22sts × 34 rows to 10cm/4in × 10cm/4in over stocking-stitch pattern, using 3.5mm needles (please note that this stocking-stitch tension is given for reference, for swatching only)
Use larger or smaller needles as necessary to obtain correct tension.

Pattern Notes

Order of construction: The shawl begins with the centre square. After completing the square, each rectangular wing is worked, one at a time. Stitches for each wing are picked up along one vertical side of the square.
Managing yarn: As Yarn A and Yarn B are used alternately throughout the shawl, to avoid having to repeatedly cut the yarn, loosely carry the end not in use up the side of the work, twisting it together with the working end at the start of the row; be careful not to pull this stranded yarn too tightly, to avoid reducing the elasticity of the shawl's edges. Alternatively, if preferred, Yarn A can be cut when switching to using Yarn B, and vice versa, and the resulting yarn ends can later be woven into the adjacent stitches of the same colour on the wrong side of the work. However, it is strongly recommended that you do not repeatedly cut the yarn ends – developing an efficient and tidy technique to twist and therefore catch in the yarn not in use is a very handy skill.

Special Abbreviation

sk2po: slip 1st, k2tog, pass slipped st over – slip the next stitch from the left-hand needle to the right-hand needle knitwise, knit the next two stitches together (k2tog), and pass the slipped stitch over the first stitch on the right-hand needle (2sts dec'd).

Pattern Instructions

Centre square

Centre-square pattern detail of the Riverside Shawl.

Left-side rectangular wing and centre-square details of the Riverside Shawl.

Set-up
Using Yarn A and 3.5mm needles, cast on 89sts.
Row 1 (RS): Purl.
Row 2 (WS): Knit.
Rows 3–4: Purl.

Chevron-Pattern Section 1
Row 1 (RS): Using Yarn B, k2, k2tog, yo, k1, yo, k10, sk2po, k10, *yo, k1, yo, sk2po, yo, k1, yo, k10, sk2po, k10; rep from * to last 5sts, yo, k1, yo, ssk, k2.
Row 2 (WS): Using Yarn B, k3, p to last 3sts, k3.
Rows 3–8: Using Yarn B, work as rows 1–2.
Row 9 (increase and decrease row): Using Yarn A, k4, yo, k1, yo, k8, k2tog, sk2po, ssk, k8, *yo, k1, yo, k3, yo, k1, yo, k8, k2tog, sk2po, ssk, k8; rep from * to last 5sts, yo, k1, yo, k4.
Row 10: Using Yarn A, knit.
Rows 11–12: Using Yarn A, work as row 2.

Chevron-Pattern Section 2
Row 1 (RS): Using Yarn B, k2, k2tog, k1, yo, k1, yo, k9, sk2po, k9, *(yo, k1) twice, sk2po, (k1, yo) twice, k9, sk2po, k9; rep from * to last 6sts, (yo, k1) twice, ssk, k2.
Rows 2–8: Using Yarn B, work as Section 1 rows 2–8.
Row 9 (increase and decrease row): Using Yarn A, k5, yo, k1, yo, k7, k2tog, sk2po, ssk, k7, *yo, k1, yo, k5, yo, k1, yo, k7, k2tog, sk2po, ssk, k7; rep from * to last 6sts, yo, k1, yo, k5.
Rows 10–12: Using Yarn A, work as Section 1 rows 10–12.

Chevron-Pattern Section 3
Row 1 (RS): Using Yarn B, k2, k2tog, k2, yo, k1, yo, k8, sk2po, k8, *yo, k1, yo, k2, sk2po, k2, yo, k1, yo, k8, sk2po, k8; rep from * to last 7sts, yo, k1, yo, k2, ssk, k2.
Rows 2–8: Using Yarn B, work as Section 1 rows 2–8.
Row 9 (increase and decrease row): Using Yarn A, k6, yo, k1, yo, k6, k2tog, sk2po, ssk, k6, *yo, k1, yo, k7, yo, k1, yo, k6, k2tog, sk2po, ssk, k6; rep from * to last 7sts, yo, k1, yo, k6.
Rows 10–12: Using Yarn A, work as Section 1 rows 10–12.

Chevron-Pattern Section 4
Row 1 (RS): Using Yarn B, k2, k2tog, k3, yo, k1, yo, k7, sk2po, k7, *yo, k1, yo, k3, sk2po, k3, yo, k1, yo, k7, sk2po, k7; rep from * to last 8sts, yo, k1, yo, k3, ssk, k2.
Rows 2–8: Using Yarn B, work as Section 1 rows 2–8.

Row 9 (increase and decrease row): Using Yarn A, k7, yo, k1, yo, k5, k2tog, sk2po, ssk, k5, *yo, k1, yo, k9, yo, k1, yo, k5, k2tog, sk2po, ssk, k5; rep from * to last 8sts, yo, k1, yo, k7.
Rows 10–12: Using Yarn A, work as Section 1 rows 10–12.

Chevron-Pattern Section 5
Row 1 (RS): Using Yarn B, k2, k2tog, k4, yo, k1, yo, k6, sk2po, k6, *yo, k1, yo, k4, sk2po, k4, yo, k1, yo, k6, sk2po, k6; rep from * to last 9sts, yo, k1, yo, k4, ssk, k2.
Rows 2–8: Using Yarn B, work as Section 1 rows 2–8.
Row 9 (increase and decrease row): Using Yarn A, k8, yo, k1, yo, k4, k2tog, sk2po, ssk, k4, *yo, k1, yo, k11, yo, k1, yo, k4, k2tog, sk2po, ssk, k4; rep from * to last 9sts, yo, k1, yo, k8.
Rows 10–12: Using Yarn A, work as Section 1 rows 10–12.

Chevron-Pattern Section 6
Row 1 (RS): Using Yarn B, k2, k2tog, k5, *yo, k1, yo, k5, sk2po, k5; rep from * to last 10sts, yo, k1, yo, k5, ssk, k2.
Rows 2–8: Using Yarn B, work as Section 1 rows 2–8.
Row 9 (increase and decrease row): Using Yarn A, k9, yo, k1, yo, k3, k2tog, sk2po, ssk, k3, *yo, k1, yo, k13, yo, k1, yo, k3, k2tog, sk2po, ssk, k3; rep from * to last 10sts, yo, k1, yo, k9.
Rows 10–12: Using Yarn A, work as Section 1 rows 10–12.

Chevron-Pattern Section 7
Row 1 (RS): Using Yarn B, k2, k2tog, k6, yo, k1, yo, k4, sk2po, k4, *yo, k1, yo, k6, sk2po, k6, yo, k1, yo, k4, sk2po, k4; rep from * to last 11sts, yo, k1, yo, k6, ssk, k2.
Rows 2–8: Using Yarn B, work as Section 1 rows 2–8.
Row 9 (increase and decrease row): Using Yarn A, k10, yo, k1, yo, k2, k2tog, sk2po, ssk, k2, *yo, k1, yo, k15, yo, k1, yo, k2, k2tog, sk2po, ssk, k2; rep from * to last 11sts, yo, k1, yo, k10.
Rows 10–12: Using Yarn A, work as Section 1 rows 10–12.

Chevron-Pattern Section 8
Row 1 (RS): Using Yarn B, k2, k2tog, k7, yo, k1, yo, k3, sk2po, k3, *yo, k1, yo, k7, sk2po, k7, yo, k1, yo, k3, sk2po, k3; rep from * to last 12sts, yo, k1, yo, k7, ssk, k2.
Rows 2–8: Using Yarn B, work as Section 1 rows 2–8.
Row 9 (increase and decrease row): Using Yarn A, k11, (yo, k1) twice, k2tog, sk2po, ssk, k1, *yo, k1, yo, k17, (yo,

k1) twice, k2tog, sk2po, ssk, k1; rep from * to last 12sts, yo, k1, yo, k11.

Rows 10–12: Using Yarn A, work as Section 1 rows 10–12.

Chevron-Pattern Section 9

Row 1 (RS): Using Yarn B, k2, k2tog, k8, yo, k1, yo, k2, sk2po, k2, *yo, k1, yo, k8, sk2po, k8, yo, k1, yo, k2, sk2po, k2; rep from * to last 13sts, yo, k1, yo, k8, ssk, k2.

Rows 2–8: Using Yarn B, work as Section 1 rows 2–8.

Row 9 (increase and decrease row): Using Yarn A, k12, yo, k1, yo, k2tog, sk2po, ssk, *yo, k1, yo, k19, yo, k1, yo, k2tog, sk2po, ssk; rep from * to last 13sts, yo, k1, yo, k12.

Rows 10–12: Using Yarn A, work as Section 1 rows 10–12.

Chevron-Pattern Section 10

Row 1 (RS): Using Yarn B, k2, k2tog, k9, (yo, k1) twice, sk2po, k1, *yo, k1, yo, k9, sk2po, k9, (yo, k1) twice, sk2po, k1; rep from * to last 14sts, yo, k1, yo, k9, ssk, k2.

Rows 2–8: Using Yarn B, work as Section 1 rows 2–8.

Row 9 (decrease row): Using Yarn A, k2, k2tog, k9, yo, k1, yo, sl2, k3tog, pass 2 slipped sts over, *yo, k1, yo, k9, sk2po, k9, yo, k1, yo, sl2, k3tog, pass 2 slipped sts over; rep from * to last 14sts, yo, k1, yo, k9, ssk, k2. (83sts, with 6sts dec'd)

Row 10: Using Yarn A, knit.

Row 11: Using Yarn A, work as Section 1 row 2.

Using Yarn A, cast off in pattern as set by Section 1 row 2.

Rectangle wings (both alike)

Set-up

With RS facing, using Yarn A and 3.5mm needles, pick up and knit 89sts along one vertical side of centre square.

Row 1 (WS): Using Yarn A, knit.

Rows 2–3: Using Yarn A, sl1, k2, p to last 3sts, k3.

Chevron-Pattern Section 1

Row 1 (RS): Using Yarn B, sl1, k1, k2tog, k5, yo, k1, yo, k5, sk2po, k5, *yo, k1, yo, k5, sk2po, k5, yo, k1, yo, k5, sk2po, k5; rep from * to last 10sts, yo, k1, yo, k5, ssk, k2.

Row 2 (WS): Using Yarn B, sl1, k2, p to last 3sts, k3.

Rows 3–8: Using Yarn B, work as rows 1–2.

The Riverside Shawl with unfolded rectangular wings.

Row 9: Using Yarn A, sl1, k to end.

Row 10: Using Yarn A, sl1, k to end.

Rows 11–12: Using Yarn A, work as row 2.

The previous 12 rows set the pattern for Section 1.

Next, work these 12 rows another two times.

Next, work rows 1–8.

Row 45 (increase row): Using Yarn A, sl1, k1, k2tog, k5, yo, k1, yo, k13, *yo, k1, yo, k5, sk2po, k5, yo, k1, yo, k13; rep from * to last 10sts, yo, k1, yo, k5, ssk, k2. (95sts, with 6sts inc'd)

Rows 46–48: Using Yarn A, work as rows 10–12.

Chevron-Pattern Section 3

Note: In the following sections, where the instructions refer to Section 1 rows, use Yarn A in place of Yarn B as the main shade, and use Yarn B in place of Yarn A to work the reverse-stocking-stitch stripes.

Row 1 (RS): Using Yarn A, sl1, k1, k2tog, k5, yo, k1, yo, k7, sk2po, k7, *yo, k1, yo, k5, sk2po, k5, yo, k1, yo, k7, sk2po, k7; rep from * to last 10sts, yo, k1, yo, k5, ssk, k2.

Rows 2–44: Using Yarns A and B as required (*see note above*), work as Section 1 rows 2–44.

Row 45 (increase row): Using Yarn B, sl1, k1, k2tog, k5, yo, k1, yo, k17, *yo, k1, yo, k5, sk2po, k5, yo, k1, yo, k17; rep from * to last 10sts, yo, k1, yo, k5, ssk, k2. (107sts, with 6sts inc'd)

Rows 46–48: Using Yarn B, work as Section 1 rows 46–48.

Chevron-Pattern Section 4

Row 1 (RS): Using Yarn A, sl1, k1, k2tog, k5, yo, k1, yo, k8, sk2po, k8, *yo, k1, yo, k5, sk2po, k5, yo, k1, yo, k8, sk2po, k8; rep from * to last 10sts, yo, k1, yo, k5, ssk, k2.

Row 2: Using Yarn A, sl1, k2, p to last 3sts, k3.

Rows 3–8: Using Yarn A, work as rows 1–2.

Row 9 (increase row): Using Yarn B, sl1, k1, k2tog, k5, yo, k1, yo, k19, *yo, k1, yo, k5, sk2po, k5, yo, k1, yo, k19; rep from * to last 10sts, yo, k1, yo, k5, ssk, k2. (113sts, with 6sts inc'd)

Row 10: Using Yarn B, sl1, k to end.

Rows 11–12: Using Yarn B, work as row 2.

Chevron-Pattern Section 5

Row 1 (RS): Using Yarn A, sl1, k1, k2tog, k5, yo, k1, yo, k9, sk2po, k9, *yo, k1, yo, k5, sk2po, k5, yo, k1, yo, k9, sk2po, k9; rep from * to last 10sts, yo, k1, yo, k5, ssk, k2.

Row 2: Using Yarn A, sl1, k2, p to last 3sts, k3.

Rows 3–8: Using Yarn A, work as rows 1–2.

Row 9 (increase row): Using Yarn B, sl1, k1, k2tog, k5, yo, k1, yo, k21, *yo, k1, yo, k5, sk2po, k5, yo, k1, yo, k21; rep from * to last 10sts, yo, k1, yo, k5, ssk, k2. (119sts, with 6sts inc'd)

Row 10: Using Yarn B, sl1, k to end.

Rows 11–12: Using Yarn B, work as row 2.

Chevron-Pattern Section 6 – border ridge

Row 1 (RS): Using Yarn A, sl1, k1, k2tog, k5, yo, k1, yo, k10,

The Riverside Shawl with folded-over rectangular wings.

Chevron-Pattern Section 2

Row 1 (RS): Using Yarn B, sl1, k1, k2tog, k5, yo, k1, yo, k6, sk2po, k6, *yo, k1, yo, k5, sk2po, k5, yo, k1, yo, k6, sk2po, k6; rep from * to last 10sts, yo, k1, yo, k5, ssk, k2.

Rows 2–44: Work as Section 1 rows 2–44.

Row 45 (increase row): Using Yarn A, sl1, k1, k2tog, k5, yo, k1, yo, k15, *yo, k1, yo, k5, sk2po, k5, yo, k1, yo, k15; rep from * to last 10sts, yo, k1, yo, k5, ssk, k2. (101sts, with 6sts inc'd)

Rows 46–48: Using Yarn A, work as Section 1 rows 46–48.

sk2po, k10, *yo, k1, yo, k5, sk2po, k5, yo, k1, yo, k10, sk2po, k10; rep from * to last 10sts, yo, k1, yo, k5, ssk, k2.

Row 2: Using Yarn A, sl1, k2, p to last 3sts, k3.

Row 3: Using Yarn A, work as row 1.

Row 4: Using Yarn A, sl1, k to end.

Row 5: Using Yarn A, work as row 2.

Using Yarn A, cast off knitwise with WS facing.

Work the second wing as for the first, from Set-Up to end of Chevron-Pattern Section 6.

Finishing

Sew in all loose ends by weaving these ends into stitches of the same colour only on the wrong side of the work, to help to avoid the contrast-colour ends showing through to the right side. Block work to measurements given and according to instructions on yarn ball bands.

CHAPTER 10

CARDIFF BAY SHAWL

Design Details

Inspiration

The Cardiff Bay area is a wonderful place to find knitting inspiration and to explore colour, texture and pattern on many different scales. The view across the bay is ever-changing, along with the weather, with sun and showers changing the colours and definition of the open water. The public areas contain both historic and modern buildings surrounded by beautiful open spaces. The Cardiff Bay Shawl is inspired by the textures and colours surrounding the Welsh National Assembly building in Cardiff, Wales. As well as by looking out across the bay and up to the rooftops of the surrounding buildings, a great deal of inspiration can be found by looking down at the ground; in this case, a small section of paving provides the detailed inspiration for the stitch patterns. The resulting shawl design combines texture and openwork to represent the intersecting paving patterns.

Shape

The overall shape of this shawl is a large triangle composed of two smaller triangles. The shape has been altered at the outer points by short-row shaping. This technique adds partial rows to specific areas

ABOVE: The Welsh Assembly Building, Cardiff, UK.

OPPOSITE: Paving detail, Cardiff Bay, UK.

RIGHT: The Cardiff Bay Shawl.

Swatch Information

Inspiration: Paving, Cardiff Bay, Wales
Shape: Triangle
Increase: Yo × 4 on RS rows
Decreases: K2tog and ssk in pattern
Start: Garter-stitch tab
End: Cast-off border
Border (top edge): Garter stitch
Border (cast-off edge): Short-row shaping and eyelets
Test yarn shown: Carol Feller (Stolen Stitches) Nua Sport (60-per-cent merino wool, 20-per-cent yak, 20-per-cent linen, 140m/153yd per 50g ball) Shade 9814 (Broken Tiles); 1 × 50g ball, approximately 20g required for swatch
Needles: A pair 4mm (UK 8/US 6) knitting needles

The Cardiff Bay swatch, knitted with 4mm needles and Carol Feller Nua Sport yarn.

Swatch Instructions

Refer to main Cardiff Bay Shawl Pattern Instructions throughout.
Use yarn of choice with appropriate needle size.
Work swatch as for Pattern Instructions for Garter-Stitch Tab to Shawl-Body Pattern B Ridges sections. (80sts)
Next, work rows 1–3 of Shawl Border. (88sts)
Next, cast off knitwise.
Block swatch according to instructions on yarn ball band.

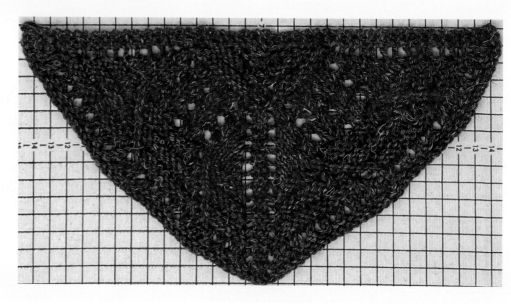

and extends the straight lines of the triangle shape to curved points. The effect of the pattern orientation is extremely important in this shawl design. Triangular tab-to-point shawls are often knitted with mirror-imaged, symmetrical stitch patterns on each side of the shawl's central spine. For the Cardiff Bay Shawl, rather than using a mirror-imaged pattern, the stitch pattern is worked in the same direction on both sides of the shawl spine. This creates a sense of movement within the pattern, with the straight-line feature on the right-hand side of the shawl appearing at right angles to that on the left-hand side. Asymmetry in design, such as in this example, draws the eye and creates interest in the pattern.

Design development

If you look closely at the detail photo of the paving, the elements that stand out include the regular grid structures and the raised bumps set within rectangular blocks of paving. The interesting angle of the corner join between sections is also a fascinating feature.

The resulting stitch pattern gradually grows outwards and downwards from a garter-stitch tab. Once the desired shawl depth is reached, the final border sections are added by using short-row shaping. The edging is completed with an eyelet border.

Yarn and swatching

A wide variety of yarns would be suitable for working this shawl design. Knitting one or more small swatches is the best way to test the stitch pattern in a variety of yarns before beginning the whole shawl project. The example test swatch shown is knitted in Carol Feller Nua Sport yarn. The flecked effect of combination of the linen and yak fibres can be seen in the swatch image and adds a textural element to the pattern.

Brooklyn Tweed Peerie fingering-weight yarn was chosen for the final shawl pattern. This pure-wool yarn creates great stitch definition, emphasizing the raised ridges of the design. To achieve a lightweight knitted fabric with drape, a larger needle size is used than the ball-band-stated needle size.

The Cardiff Bay Shawl, opened out.

Cardiff Bay Shawl Pattern

The Cardiff Bay Shawl, folded.

Size

65cm/25½in (centre depth) × 121cm/47¾in (straight top edge)

Yarns

Brooklyn Tweed Peerie (100-per-cent American merino wool, 192m/210yd per 50g ball)
Yarn A: Nocturne; 2 × 50g skeins
Yarn B: Mesa; 2 × 50g skeins
Yarn amounts given are based on average requirements and are approximate.

Accessories

A pair 4mm (UK 8/US 6) knitting needles
Stitch markers – 4

Tensions

12sts × 12 rows to 5cm/2in × 4cm/1½in over Pattern A, using 4mm needles
12sts × 12 rows to 5cm/2in × 3cm/1¼in over Pattern B, using 4mm needles

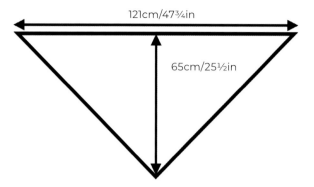

121cm/47¾in

65cm/25½in

Blocking diagram for the Cardiff Bay Shawl.

24sts × 30 rows to 10cm/4in × 10cm/4in over stocking-stitch pattern, using 4mm needles
Use larger or smaller needles as necessary to obtain correct tension.

Pattern Notes

Garter-stitch tab: The shawl begins with a garter-stitch tab and is worked top down from this tab.
Increases: The shawl stitches are increased by four on every RS row, with one stitch being increased at the beginning and at the end of every row and two stitches being increased on each side of the central spine.
Stitch markers: Stitch markers are used to set the stitch-pattern placements; on subsequent rows after a marker is placed, when the marker is reached, slip the marker purlwise from the left-hand needle to the right-hand needle. Stitch markers are placed at the start of and removed at the end of each 12-row pattern section.
Short-row (SR) shaping: Short-row shaping is used to create the shaping of the lower edge of the shawl.

A stitch is wrapped to avoid a gap remaining in the knitting where each short row is worked. This wrapping action is known as wrap and turn, 'w&t'. For this pattern, to wrap a stitch, knit to the stitch to be wrapped; slip the next stitch purlwise; take the yarn to the back of the work; slip the slipped stitch back to the left-hand needle purlwise without working it; take the yarn to the front of the work; and turn the work. When the wrapped stitch is reached on the subsequent row, work the wrap loop and the wrapped stitch together to close the gap between the wrapped stitch and the adjacent stitch.

Stitch Patterns

Use charted or written patterns, as preferred.

Pattern A, worked over 12sts and 4 rows
Row 1 (RS): K2tog, yo twice, ssk, k4, k2tog, yo twice, ssk.
Row 2 (WS): P1, k1, p7, k1, p2.
Row 3: K4, k2tog, yo twice, ssk, k4.
Row 4: P5, k1, p6.

Pattern B, worked over 12sts and 12 rows
Row 1 (RS): P3, k2tog, yo twice, ssk, p5.
Row 2 (WS): K5, p1, k1, p2, k3.
Row 3: K4, k2tog, yo twice, ssk, k4.
Row 4: P5, k1, p6.
Row 5: P5, k2tog, yo twice, ssk, p3.
Row 6: K3, p1, k1, p2, k5.
Row 7: K6, k2tog, yo twice, ssk, k2.
Row 8: P3, k1, p8.
Row 9: P7, k2tog, yo twice, ssk, p1.

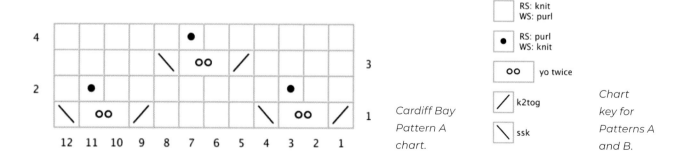

Cardiff Bay Pattern A chart.

☐	RS: knit WS: purl
●	RS: purl WS: knit
oo	yo twice
╱	k2tog
╲	ssk

Chart key for Patterns A and B.

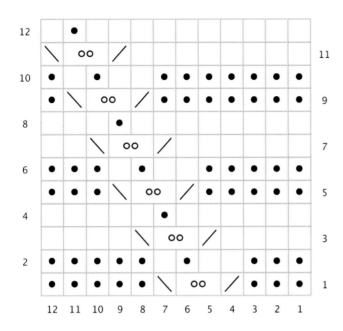

Row 10: K1, p1, k1, p2, k7.
Row 11: K8, k2tog, yo twice, ssk.
Row 12: P1, k1, p10.

Pattern Instructions

Garter-stitch tab
Using Yarn A and 4mm needles, cast on 3sts.

Detail of the centre back of the Cardiff Bay Shawl.

Cardiff Bay Pattern B chart.

Asymmetric stitch-pattern detail of the Cardiff Bay Shawl.

Knit 7 rows. After working the seventh row (RS), do not turn work.
Next, with 3sts on right-hand needle, pick up and knit 2sts along side of tab and 3sts along cast-on edge. (8sts)
Next row (WS): Sl1, k to end.

Ridge set-up
Row 1 (RS): Sl1, *k2, yo twice; rep from * to last 3sts, k3. (12sts)
Row 2 (WS): Sl1, *k3, p1; rep from * to last 3sts, k3.
Row 3: Sl1, *k2, yo; rep from * to last 3sts, k3. (16sts)
Row 4: Sl1, *k2, p4; rep from * to last 3sts, k3.
Row 5: Sl1, *k2, yo, p4, yo; rep from * to last 3sts, k3. (20sts)
Row 6: Sl1, k to end.
Row 7: Sl1, *k2, yo, k6, yo; rep from * to last 3sts, k3. (24sts)
Row 8: Sl1, *k2, p8; rep from* to last 3sts, k3.
Row 9: Sl1, *k2, yo, p8, yo; rep from * to last 3sts, k3. (28sts)

Row 10: Work as row 6.
Row 11: Sl1, *k2, yo, k10, yo; rep from * to last 3sts, k3. (32sts)
Row 12: Sl1, *k2, p12; rep from * to last 3sts, k3.

Pattern A set-up
Row 1 (RS, placing 5 stitch markers): Sl1, k2, yo, pm, work Pattern A row 1, pm, yo, k1, pm (centre mrk), k1, yo, pm, work Pattern A row 1, pm, yo, k3. (36sts)
Row 2 (WS): Sl1, k2, p to first mrk, work Pattern A row 2, p to 1st before centre mrk, k2, p to fourth mrk, work Pattern A row 2, p to last 3sts, k3.
Row 3: Sl1, k2, yo, k to first mrk, work Pattern A row 3, k to 1st before centre mrk, yo, k2, yo, k to fourth mrk, work Pattern A row 3, k to last 3sts, yo, k3. (40sts)
Row 4: Sl1, k2, p to first mrk, work Pattern A row 4, p to 1st before centre mrk, k2, p to fourth mrk, work Pattern A row 4, p to last 3sts, k3.
Row 5: Sl1, k2, yo, k to first mrk, work Pattern A row 1, k to 1st before centre mrk, yo, k2, yo, k to fourth mrk, work Pattern A row 1, k to last 3sts, yo, k3. (44sts)
The previous 4 rows set the placement of Pattern A.
Rows 6–9: Work as rows 2–5. (52sts after row 9 has been completed)
Rows 10–12: Work as rows 2–4. (56sts after row 12 has been completed)
Leaving centre marker in place, remove first, second, fourth and fifth markers.

Shawl body

Pattern B ridges
Row 1 (RS, placing 4 stitch markers): Sl1, k2, yo, pm, *work Pattern B row 1; rep from * to 1st before centre mrk, pm, yo, k2, yo, pm, *work Pattern B row 1; rep from * to last 3sts, pm, yo, k3. (60sts)
Row 2 (WS): Sl1, k to first mrk, *work Pattern B row 2; rep from * to second mrk, k to fourth mrk, *work Pattern B row 2; rep from * to fifth mrk, k to end.
Row 3: Sl1, k2, yo, k to first mrk, *work Pattern B row 3; rep from * to second mrk, k to 1st before centre mrk, yo, k2, yo, k to fourth mrk, *work Pattern B row 3; rep from * to fifth mrk, k to last 3sts, yo, k3. (64sts)
Row 4: Sl1, k2, p to first mrk, *work Pattern B row 4; rep from * to second mrk, p to 1st before centre mrk, k2, p

to fourth mrk, *work Pattern B row 4; rep from * to fifth mrk, p to last 3sts, k3.
Row 5: Sl1, k2, yo, p to first mrk, *work Pattern B row 5; rep from * to second mrk, p to 1st before centre mrk, yo, k2, yo, p to fourth mrk, *work Pattern B row 5; rep from * to fifth mrk, p to last 3sts, yo, k3. (68sts)
Row 6: Sl1, k to first mrk, *work Pattern B row 6; rep from * to second mrk, k to fourth mrk, *work Pattern B row 6; rep from * to fifth mrk, k to end.
Rows 7–10: Work as set by rows 3–6, using Pattern B rows 7–10. (76sts when row 10 has been completed)
Rows 11–12: Work as set by rows 3–4, using Pattern B rows 11–12. (80sts when row 12 has been completed)
Leaving centre marker in place, remove first, second, fourth and fifth markers.

Pattern A lattice
Row 1 (RS, placing 4 stitch markers): Sl1, k2, yo, pm, *work Pattern A row 1, k12; rep from * to 13sts before centre mrk, work pattern A row 1, pm, yo, k2, yo, pm, *work Pattern A row 1, k12; rep from * to last 15sts, work pattern A row 1, pm, yo, k3. (84sts)
Row 2 (WS): Sl1, k2, p to first mrk, *work Pattern A row 2, p12; rep from * to 12sts before second mrk, work Pattern A row 2, p to 1st before centre mrk, k2, p to fourth mrk, *work Pattern A row 2, p12; rep from * to 12sts before fifth mrk, work Pattern A row 2, p to last 3sts, k to end.
Row 3: Sl1, k2, yo, k to first mrk, *work Pattern A row 3, k12; rep from * to 12sts before second mrk, work Pattern A row 3, p to 1st before centre mrk, yo, k2, yo, p to fourth mrk, *work Pattern A row 3, k12; rep from * to 12sts before fifth mrk, work Pattern A row 3, k to last 3sts, yo, k3. (88sts)
Row 4: Sl1, k2, p to first mrk, *work Pattern A row 4, p12; rep from * to 12sts before second mrk, work Pattern A row 4, p to 1st before centre mrk, k2, p to fourth mrk, *work Pattern A row 4, p12; rep from * to 12sts before fifth mrk, work Pattern A row 4, p to last 3sts, k3.
Row 5: Sl1, k2, yo, k to first mrk, *work Pattern A row 1, k12; rep from * to 12sts before second mrk, work Pattern A row 1, p to 1st before centre mrk, yo, k2, yo, p to fourth mrk, *work Pattern A row 1, k12; rep from * to 12sts before fifth mrk, work Pattern A row 1, k to last 3sts, yo, k3. (92sts)
The previous 4 rows set the placement of the Pattern A Lattice.

Rows 6–9: Work as rows 2–5. (100sts after row 9 has been completed)

Rows 10–12: Work as rows 2–4. (104sts after row 12 has been completed)

Leaving centre marker in place, remove first, second, fourth and fifth markers.

The previous 24 rows set the shawl-body pattern, with alternating 12-row sections of Pattern B Ridges and Pattern A Lattice.

Next, work these 24 rows another two times, until Pattern A Lattice row 12 has been completed. (200sts)

Next, using Yarn B, work all 12 rows of Pattern B Ridges. (224sts)

Next, using Yarn A, work all 12 rows of Pattern A Lattice. (248sts)

The previous 24 rows set the stripe pattern.

Next, work these 24 rows once. (296sts)

Next, using Yarn B, work all 12 rows of Pattern B Ridges. (320sts)

Next, using Yarn B, work all 12 rows of Pattern A Lattice. (344sts)

Leaving centre marker in place, remove first, second, fourth and fifth markers.

Shawl points

Left-point SR section

SR1 (RS): Sl1, k2, yo, k55, w&t; (345sts, with 1st inc'd)

SR2 (WS): K to end.

SR3: Sl1, k2, yo, k to 10sts before last wrap, w&t; (346sts, with 1st inc'd)

SR4: K to end.

SR5–12: Work as SRs3–4. (350sts, with 4sts inc'd)

SR13: Sl1, k2, yo, k to 5sts before last wrap, w&t; (351sts, with 1st inc'd)

SR14: K to end.

Centre-point SR section

SR1 (RS): Sl1, k2, yo, k to 1st before mrk, yo, k2, yo, k55, w&t. (354sts, with 3sts inc'd)

SR2 (WS): K to 57sts after mrk, w&t;

SR3: K to 1st before mrk, yo, k2, yo, k to 10sts before last wrap, w&t; (356sts, with 2sts inc'd)

SR4: K to 10sts before last wrap, w&t;

SR5–12: Work as SRs3–4. (364sts, with 8sts inc'd)

Detail of a shaped point of the Cardiff Bay Shawl.

SR13: K to 1st before mrk, yo, k2, yo, k to 5sts before last wrap, w&t; (366sts, with 2sts inc'd)

SR14: K to 5sts before last wrap, w&t;

SR15: K to 1st before mrk, yo, k2, yo, k to last 3sts, yo, k3. (369sts, with 3sts inc'd)

Right-point SR section

SR1 (WS): Sl1, k58, w&t;

SR2 (RS): K to last 3sts, yo, k3. (370sts, with 1st inc'd)

SR3: Sl1, k to 10sts before last wrap, w&t;

SR4: K to last 3sts, yo, k3. (371sts, with 1st inc'd)

SR5–12: Work as SRs3–4. (375sts, with 4sts inc'd)

SR13: Sl1, k to 5sts before last wrap, w&t;

SR14: K to last 3sts, yo, k3. (376sts, with 1st inc'd)

SR15: Sl1, k to end.

Shawl border

Row 1 (RS): Sl1, k2, yo, k1, *yo, k2tog; rep from * to 2sts before mrk, k1, yo, k2, yo, k1, *k2tog, yo; rep from * to last 4sts, k1, yo, k3. (380sts, with 4sts inc'd)

Row 2 (WS): Sl1, k to end.

Row 3: Sl1, k2, yo, k to 1st before mrk, yo, k2, yo, k to last 3sts, yo, k3. (384sts, with 4sts inc'd)

Cast off knitwise with WS facing.

Finishing

Sew in all loose ends. Block work to measurements given and according to instructions on yarn ball bands.

CHAPTER 11

MODERNISM SHAWL

Design Details

Inspiration

Architecture is a wonderful source of inspiration for knitting designs. Looking at particular styles of architecture can spark many ideas. This shawl design is inspired by a building constructed in a style known as 'desert modern'. This type of architecture can be found throughout the Californian city of Palm Springs.

In old-town Palm Springs, the Welmas Building, designed by renowned architects Donald Wexler (1926–2015) and Richard Harrison (1921–1993) in 1959, is a commercial building situated at 201–267 E. Tahquitz Canyon Way. Aspects of this building are the inspiration for the Modernism Shawl, in particular the staircase and the outer building tiles.

The shawl pattern combines a distinctive stepped edging pattern with a grid-like texture, representing the tiles. The grid is defined by raised ridges of reverse stocking stitch with intersecting smooth centres of stocking stitch. The grid pattern extends into the centre section of the shawl with the addition of an alternating textured-tile pattern. The different sections of the shawl are all unified by the tile pattern and the stepped edging pattern that runs along the entire outer curved border.

OPPOSITE: The Welmas Building staircase inspired the Modernism Shawl.

Sketch of the Welmas Building staircase.

Shape

The overall shape of this shawl can be described as a crescent, as the shawl appears to have a curving outer edge with long points on each side of the central section.

This crescent is constructed from two triangles separated by a rectangle. The first triangle is worked at the start of the shawl. Increases are worked near the beginning of every right-side row until the desired shawl width is reached. At this stage, the shawl continues as a rectangle, with no further increases regularly being made throughout this section. Once the desired shawl length has been reached, the second triangle begins. This time, decreases are worked near the beginning of every right-side row. The decreases continue until the second point of the triangle is reached.

Design development

The design for the Modernism Shawl has been developed in stages. The first step was to focus on the border. This was identified as the key part of the design. Using the staircase as the starting point, increasing and decreasing were used to form angled sections of knitting. A bold textural element was added by including reverse-stocking-stitch ridges. The stitches for the start of the first triangle were cast on; these stitches were then decreased over the following rows. The process was repeated, forming a line of triangles set in a horizontal band.

The second step was to link the border to the main pattern to be used for the shawl body. For this experimental swatch, the textured ridges and contrasting stocking-stitch sections of the border triangles were extended to form a series of tiles. The two sections of the shawl were divided by a two-stitch raised-rib section.

The third main development was to place the border at an angle, reflecting the angle of the staircase, and to consider how the tile pattern might emerge from this angle. For this experiment, the raised ridges originating from the ends of the border triangles were knitted in a contrasting yarn shade. This helped to identify how the component parts of the design would interact with each other.

The final part of the development was to test the ideas all together in a small shawl swatch. This swatch tested all of the components to be included in the final pattern. These are the triangular border pattern, the angled shawl increases and the ridged tile pattern. Some additional components were also added, to check how a mirror-imaged decrease section would look and to test a textured pattern for the tiles.

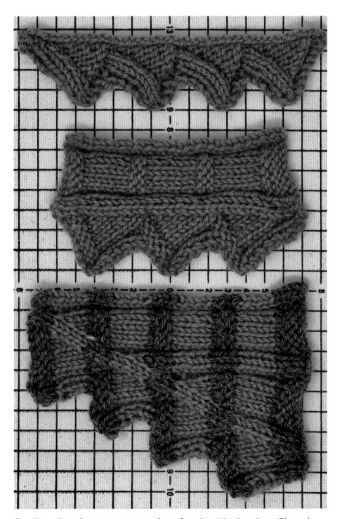

Design development swatches for the Modernism Shawl.

Yarn and swatching

The test yarn selected is from the John Arbon Textiles Knit By Numbers range. This pure-wool 4ply yarn provides excellent stitch definition, especially for the reverse-stocking-stitch ridges. For the full-size shawl, a DK/sport-weight yarn was chosen; additionally, the beautiful colour of the Welmas Building is represented by the bold raspberry shade of the chosen Garthenor Organic Beacons yarn. The yarn's stitch definition and strong structure give body to the shawl. The stitch definition is particularly important for the centre textured-tile pattern.

Elements of the test swatch have been used to

create the pattern for the full-size shawl. These include the use of offset texture in the shawl centre, where every second tile has a textured centre rather than each individual tile. Additionally, the final design has an extended rectangular centre section with no increases. This centre section contains the textured-tile pattern and is bordered on each side by the mirror-imaged increase and decrease sections. The triangular border runs along the full length of the outer edge of the shawl.

Swatch Information

Inspiration: Desert-modern architecture, Palm Springs, California
Shape: Crescent formed from two triangles and one rectangle
Increase: M1
Decreases: K2tog, ssk
Start: Tip of triangle
Centre: Rectangle
End: Tip of triangle
Border (top edge): Slipped-stitch edging
Border (outer edge): Stepped edge
Test yarn shown: John Arbon Textiles Knit By Numbers (KBN) 4ply (100-per-cent pure Falklands merino wool, 400m/437yd per 100g skein)
Shade KBN116 (brown); 1 × 50g skein, approximately 20g required for swatch
Needles: A pair 4mm (UK 8/US 6) knitting needles

Swatch Instructions

Refer to main Modernism Shawl Pattern Instructions throughout.
Use yarn of choice with appropriate needle size.

Work swatch as for Pattern Instructions for Increase Section to end of row 9 of Step 4. (31sts)
Set up for centre section as follows:
Next row (WS): Sl1, p1, k2, p8, k2, p9, m1, p to last 4sts, k2, p2. (32sts)

Next, work rows 1–20 of Centre Section. (32sts)
Next, work rows 1–20 of Decrease Section. (22sts)
Next, work rows 1–22 of Shawl Point, and fasten off.
Block swatch according to instructions on yarn ball band.

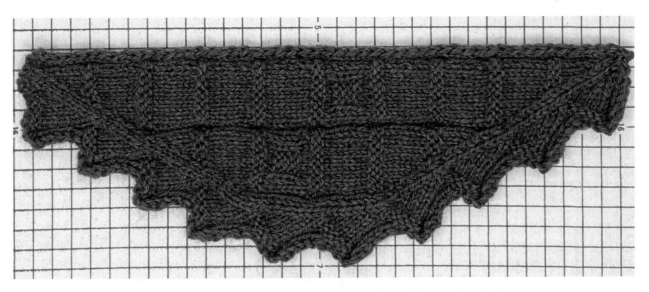

Modernism swatch, knitted with 4mm needles and John Arbon Textiles Knit By Numbers 4ply yarn.

Modernism Shawl Pattern

The Modernism Shawl.

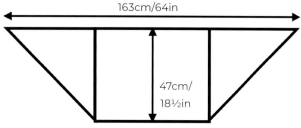

Blocking diagram for the Modernism Shawl.

Size

47cm/18½in (centre width) × 163cm/64¼in (straight top edge)

Yarn

Garthenor Organic Beacons (60-per-cent organic Polwarth from Dunbar Island, Falkland Islands, 40-per-cent Romney from Wiltshire, England, 135m/148yd per 50g ball)
Shade Raspberry; 5 × 50g skeins

Yarn amounts given are based on average requirements and are approximate.

Accessories

A pair 4mm (UK 8/US 6) knitting needles
Stitch markers – 2

Tension

24sts × 32 rows to 10cm/4in × 10cm/4in over centre-section pattern (*see* Centre Section), using 4mm needles
Use larger or smaller needles as necessary to obtain correct tension.

Pattern Notes

Stitch markers: Stitch markers are used to set the position of the decrease line and transition between stitch patterns; on subsequent rows after a marker is placed, when the marker is reached, slip the marker purlwise from the left-hand needle to the right-hand needle.
Increases: Five additional stitches are cast on at the beginning of each step of the border pattern. Five stitches are then gradually decreased over the next nine rows, to form the stepped edge. At the same time, the shawl is gradually widened by working an additional increase stitch.

Stitch Pattern (Centre Section Only)

Use charted or written pattern, as preferred.

Texture Pattern, worked over 20sts and 20 rows
Row 1 (RS): Purl.
Row 2 (WS): Knit.
Row 3: (P2, k8) × 2.
Row 4: (P8, k2) × 2.
Row 5: P2, k2, p4, k2, p2, k8.

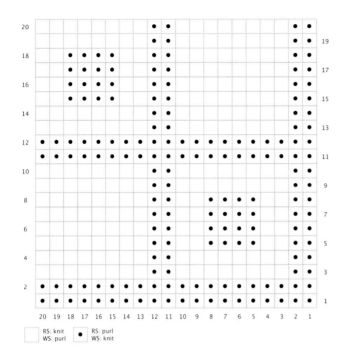

The chart shows row numbers 1–20 with column numbers 20–1 along the bottom.

RS: knit / WS: purl (white square)
RS: purl / WS: knit (black dot square)

Modernism Shawl Texture Pattern chart.

Row 6: P8, k2, p2, k4, p2, k2.
Rows 7–8: As rows 5–6.
Rows 9–10: As rows 3–4.
Row 11: Purl.
Row 12: Knit.
Rows 13–14: As rows 3–4.
Row 15: P2, k8, p2, k2, p4, k2.
Row 16: P2, k4, p2, k2, p8, k2.
Rows 17–18: As rows 15–16.
Rows 19–20: As rows 3–4.

Pattern Instructions

Increase section
Using 4mm needles, cast on 17sts.

Step 1
Row 1 (RS, placing first stitch marker): Sl1, k1, p7, k1, k2tog, pm, k1, p2, k2. (16sts, with 1st dec'd)
Row 2 (WS): Sl1, p1, k2, p3, k to last 2sts, p2.
Row 3: Sl1, k1, p2, k to 2sts before mrk, k2tog, k1, m1, p2, k2.
Row 4: Sl1, p1, k2, p to last 4sts, k2, p2.

Detail of the cast-on and increase sections of the Modernism Shawl.

Row 5: Sl1, k1, p2, k to 2sts before mrk, k2tog, k1, m1, k to last 4sts, p2, k2.
Rows 6–10: Work as rows 4–5, ending with a WS row 4.

Step 2
Row 1 (RS): Cast on 5sts at beginning of row, sl1, k1, p7, k1, k2tog, k1, m1, p to last 2sts, k2. (21sts, with 6sts inc'd and 1st dec'd)
Row 2 (WS): Sl1, p1, k to 1st before last mrk of row, p3, k to last 2sts, p2.
Rows 3–10: Work as Step 1 rows 4–5, beginning with a RS row 5.

Step 3
Rows 1–2: Work as Step 2 rows 1–2. (26sts, with 6sts inc'd and 1st dec'd when row 2 has been completed)
Row 3: Sl1, k1, p2, k to 2sts before mrk, k2tog, k1, m1, p2, k8, p2, k2.
Row 4: Sl1, p1, k2, p8, k2, p to last 4sts, k2, p2.
Row 5: Sl1, k1, p2, k to 2sts before mrk, k2tog, k1, m1, k to last 14sts, p2, k8, p2, k2.
Rows 6–10: Work as rows 4–5, ending with a WS row 4.

Step 4
Rows 1–2: Work as Step 2 rows 1–2. (31sts, with 6sts inc'd and 1st dec'd when row 2 has been completed)
Rows 3–10: Work as Step 3 rows 4–5, beginning with a RS row 5.

Step 5

Rows 1–2: Work as Step 2 rows 1–2. (36sts, with 6sts inc'd and 1st dec'd when row 2 has been completed)

Row 3 (placing second stitch marker): Sl1, k1, p2, k to 2sts before mrk, k2tog, k1, m1, pm, *p2, k8; rep from * to last 4sts, p2, k2.

Row 4: Sl1, p1, k2, *p8, k2; rep from * to mrk, p to last 4sts, k2, p2.

Row 5: Sl1, k1, p2, k to 2sts before mrk, k2tog, k1, m1, k to mrk, *p2, k8; rep from * to last 4sts, p2, k2.

Rows 6–10: Work as rows 4–5, ending with a WS row 4.

Step 6

Rows 1–2: Work as Step 2 rows 1–2. (41sts, with 6sts inc'd and 1st dec'd when row 1 has been completed)

Rows 3–9: Work as Step 5 rows 4–5, beginning and ending with a RS row 5.

Row 10 (removing first mrk and leaving second mrk of row in place): Sl1, p1, k2, *p8, k2; rep from * to mrk, remove mrk, p to last 4sts, k2, p2.

The previous 20 rows (Steps 5 and 6) set both the increase pattern and the tile pattern. Note that the stated stitch counts are relevant to only the first 20 rows of the increase and tile patterns.

Work these 20 rows another six times, incorporating an additional tile-pattern repeat for every alternate step as set as the shawl-body stitches are increased. (106sts) Next, work rows 1–19. (111sts)

Set-up for main pattern of centre section

Row 20 (WS, removing first mrk and leaving second mrk of row in place): Sl1, p1, k2, *p8, k2; rep from * to mrk, remove mrk, p9, m1, p to last 4sts, k2, p2. (112sts, with 1st inc'd)

Centre section

Row 1 (RS): Cast on 5sts at beginning of row, sl1, k1, p7, k1, k2tog, k1, *work Texture Pattern row 1; rep from * to last 4sts, p2, k2. (116sts, with 5sts inc'd and 1st dec'd)

Row 2 (WS): Sl1, p1, k2, *work Texture Pattern row 2; rep from * to 1st before mrk, p3, k to last 2sts, p2.

Row 3: Sl1, k1, p2, k to 2sts before mrk, k2tog, k1, *work Texture Pattern row 3; rep from * to last 4sts, p2, k2. (115sts, with 1st dec'd)

Row 4: Sl1, p1, k2, *work Texture Pattern row 4; rep from * to 1st before mrk, p to last 4sts, k2, p2.

Rows 5–10: Work as set by rows 3–4, using Texture Pattern rows 5–10. (112sts when row 10 has been completed, with 1st dec'd on each of rows 5, 7 and 9)

Row 11: Work as set by row 1, using Texture Pattern row 11. (116sts, with 5sts inc'd and 1st dec'd)

Rows 12–20: Work as set by rows 2–10, using Texture Pattern rows 12–20. (112sts when row 20 has been completed, with 1st dec'd on each of rows 13, 15, 17 and 19)

The previous 20 rows set the centre-section pattern.

Work these 20 rows another four times.

Next, work rows 1–10. (112sts when row 10 has been completed)

Decrease section

Row 1 (RS, leaving first mrk in place and placing second mrk): Cast on

Detail of the textured-tile centre section of the Modernism Shawl.

5sts at beginning of row, sl1, k1, p7, k1, k2tog, ssk, p9, pm, p to last 2sts, k2. (115sts, with 5sts inc'd and 2sts dec'd)

Row 2 (WS): Sl1, p1, k to 1st before last mrk of row, p3, k to last 2sts, p2.

Row 3: Sl1, k1, p2, k to 2sts before mrk, k2tog, ssk, k to mrk, *p2, k8; rep from * to last 4sts, p2, k2. (113sts, with 2sts dec'd)

Row 4: Sl1, p1, k2, *p8, k2; rep from * to mrk, p to last 4sts, k2, p2.

Rows 5–10: Work as rows 3–4. (107sts when row 10 has been completed, with 2sts dec'd on each of rows 5, 7 and 9)

Row 11: Cast on 5sts at beginning of row, sl1, k1, p7, k1, k2tog, ssk, p to last 2sts, k2. (110sts, with 5sts inc'd and 2sts dec'd)

Row 12: Work as row 2.

Rows 13–18: Work as rows 3–4. (104sts when row 18 has been completed, with 2sts dec'd on each of rows 13, 15 and 17)

Row 19: Sl1, k1, p2, k to 2sts before mrk, k2tog, ssk, *p2, k8; rep from * to last 4sts, p2, k2. (102sts when row 19 has been completed, with 2sts dec'd)

Row 20 (removing first mrk and leaving second mrk of row in place): Sl1, p1, k2, *p8, k2; rep from * to mrk, remove mrk, p to last 4sts, k2, p2.

The previous 20 rows set both the decrease pattern and the tile pattern. Note that the stated stitch counts are relevant to only the first 20 rows of the decrease and tile patterns.

Work these 20 rows another eight times. (22sts when row 20 has been completed)

Shawl point

Row 1 (RS): Cast on 5sts at beginning of row, sl1, k1, p7, k1, k2tog, ssk, p to last 2sts, k2. (25sts, with 5sts inc'd and 2sts dec'd)

Row 2 (WS): Sl1, p1, k to 1st before mrk, p3, k to last 2sts, p2.

Row 3: Sl1, k1, p2, k to 2sts before mrk, k2tog, ssk, k to last 4sts, p2, k2. (23sts, with 2sts dec'd)

Row 4: Sl1, p1, k2, p to last 4sts, k2, p2.

Rows 5–10: Work as rows 3–4. (17sts when row 10 has been completed)

Row 11: Cast on 5sts at beginning of row, sl1, k1, p7, k1,

Edging detail and one shawl point of the Modernism Shawl.

k2tog, ssk, p to last 2sts, k2. (20sts, with 5sts inc'd and 2sts dec'd)

Row 12: Work as row 2.

Rows 13–16: Work as rows 3–4. (16sts when row 16 has been completed)

Row 17: Sl1, k1, p2, k1, k2tog twice, ssk, k1, p2, k2. (13sts, with 3sts dec'd)

Row 18: Work as row 4.

Row 19: Sl1, k1, p1, k2tog twice, ssk, p2, k2. (10sts, with 3sts dec'd)

Row 20: Sl1, p1, k2tog, p2, p2tog twice. (7sts, with 3sts dec'd)

Row 21: Sl1, k2tog, ssk, k2. (5sts, with 2sts dec'd)

Row 22: Sl1, p3tog, p1. (3sts, with 2sts dec'd)

Knit the remaining 3sts together (k3tog), and fasten off.

Finishing

Sew in all loose ends. Block work gently to measurements given and according to instructions on yarn ball band.

CHAPTER 12

OPEN DOORS SHAWL

Design Details

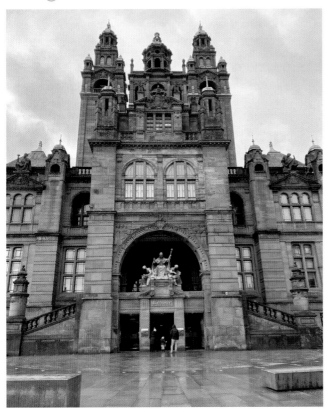

The Kelvingrove Art Gallery and Museum, Glasgow, UK.

OPPOSITE: *Detail of metal gates, designed by John Creed, at the Kelvingrove Art Gallery and Museum, Glasgow, UK.*

Inspiration

Since its opening in 1901, Glasgow's Kelvingrove Art Gallery and Museum has attracted countless visitors to its stunning galleries. Around eight-thousand objects are displayed in twenty-two galleries covering art, arms and armour, natural history and many more topics. There are inspirational objects throughout the grand and imposing red sandstone building, and every visit reveals a new treasure. Visitors can enter the building through either the street-side or the river-side entrance. John Creed's stunning metal security gates are located at the lower river-side entrance and provide the inspiration for the Open Doors Shawl.

Consisting of curved sections of textured metal, the width of each section of the gates changes over their 2.8-metre height. The gates appear different depending on the viewer's location. Standing inside, a visitor can see how the light reflects from the stainless-steel

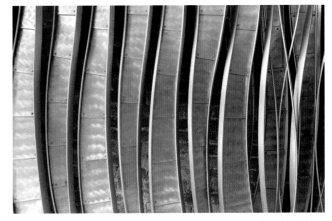

The yarn choice for the Open Doors Shawl was inspired by reflections on the metal gates at Kelvingrove Art Gallery and Museum.

Swatch Information

Inspiration: Security gates by John Creed, Kelvingrove Art Gallery and Museum, Glasgow, UK

Shape: Triangle and two rectangles

Increases: Yo, yob

Decreases: K2tog, ssk

Start: Tip of triangle

Centre: Triangle and two rectangles

End: One tip of each rectangle

Border (outer): Slipped-stitch-and-rib edging

Border (inner): Slipped-stitch-and-rib edging

Test yarn shown: Irish Artisan Yarn hand-dyed 4ply (65-per-cent superwash merino, 20-per-cent bamboo, 15-per-cent silk, 350m/383yd per 100g skein) Shade Greyabbey; 1 × 100g skein, approximately 15g required for triangular swatch of larger size

Needles: A pair 4mm (UK 8/US 6) knitting needles

Swatch Instructions (Triangular Section)

Refer to main Open Doors Shawl Pattern Instructions throughout.
Use choice of yarn with appropriate needle size.

Work swatch as for Pattern Instructions for Triangle Set-Up to end of Patterns A and B Set-Up. (35sts)
For a larger swatch (as shown), work the first 16 rows of Triangle Main Pattern (for which all rows of Patterns A and Pattern B are completed once and all rows of Patterns C and D are completed twice). (51sts)
Cast off in pattern.
Block swatch according to instructions on yarn ball band.

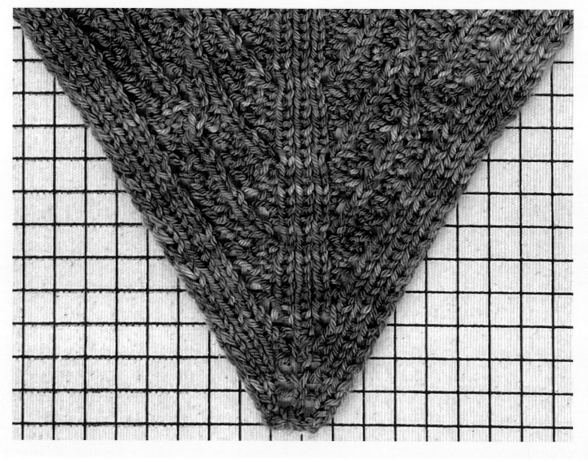

Open Doors swatch, knitted with 4mm needles and Irish Artisan Yarn hand-dyed 4ply yarn.

surface into the entrance hall. Walking outside and taking a look back towards the building, visitors see colourful reflections of the red sandstone, as well as the green of the surrounding grass. This ever-changing iridescent tint of colour is fascinating and inspired the choice of yarn for this project.

Shape

Beginning with a triangle shape, the shawl extends outwards into two rectangles. The overall shape is similar to that of a large triangle with the centre cut out in the shape of a smaller triangle.

Design development

The stitch pattern is designed to grow outwards from the centre of the triangle and then extend into the rectangles. The same stitch patterns are worked throughout the shawl sections, creating a series of straight and diagonal lines that appear to change direction and intersect in different ways. Within the triangle, the diagonals travel outwards from the centre, and the straight lines appear vertical. Within the rectangles, the pattern continues to be knitted in the same way. However, the same lines are reorientated, with the diagonals now appearing vertical and the straight lines being worked on the bias. Using the same stitch pattern within different shapes in the same shawl is a very effective design tool. The most repeated stitch patterns in this shawl are two mirror-imaged eight-stitch and eight-row blocks. The small repeat of these patterns allows the knitter to become very familiar with the pattern and comfortable with working it in different ways within the different sections of the shawl.

Yarn and swatching

The metallic stainless-steel sheen of the doors is represented by using a yarn containing silk and bamboo fibres. The reflection of the surrounding colours on the gates is represented by the hand-painted hints of colour that are placed subtly throughout the yarn.

Open Doors Shawl Pattern

Size

51cm/20in (triangle centre depth) × 102cm/40in (outer edge, from triangle point to rectangle end point) × 70cm/27½in (inner edge, from centre back of neck to rectangle end point) × 19cm/7½in (rectangle width)

The Open Doors Shawl.

Close-up of the Open Doors Shawl stitch pattern detail.

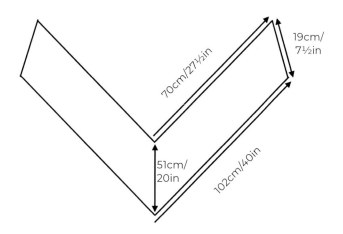

Blocking diagram for the Open Doors Shawl.

Yarn

Irish Artisan Yarn hand-dyed 4ply (65-per-cent super-wash merino, 20-per-cent bamboo, 15-per-cent silk, 350m/383yd per 100g skein)
Shade Greyabbey; 2 × 100g skeins
Yarn amounts given are based on average require-ments and are approximate.

Accessories

A pair 4mm (UK 8/US 6) knitting needles
Spare needle or stitch holder
Stitch markers – 4

Tensions

32sts × 31 rows to 10cm/4in × 10cm/4in over Pattern C and/or D, using 4mm needles
20sts × 30 rows to 10cm/4in × 10cm/4in over stocking-stitch pattern, using 4mm needles (please note that this stocking-stitch tension is given for reference, for swatching only, as this stitch pattern is not used in the shawl pattern itself)
Use larger or smaller needles to obtain correct tension.

Pattern Notes

Order of construction: The shawl begins with the triangle. After dividing the stitches for the right and

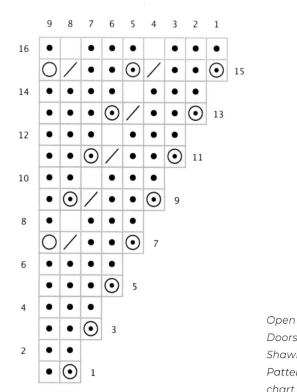

Open Doors Shawl Pattern A chart.

Open Doors Shawl Pattern B chart.

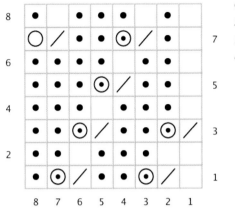

Open Doors Shawl Pattern C chart.

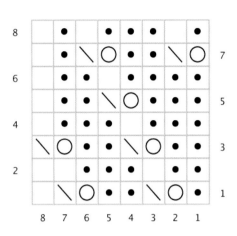

Open Doors Shawl Pattern D chart.

RS: knit WS: purl	• RS: purl WS: knit	/ k2tog	\ ssk	○ yo	⊙ yob

Chart key for Patterns A–D.

left sides of the shawl, the back-of-neck shaping is completed, and each rectangle is then worked separately on the bias.

Stitch markers: Stitch markers are used to set the stitch-pattern placements at the beginning of each 16-row pattern section; on subsequent rows after a marker is placed, when the marker is reached, slip the marker purlwise from the left-hand needle to the right-hand needle.

Special Abbreviation

yob: yarn over backwards – take the yarn over the right-hand needle from back to front (backwards) (1st inc'd); where a k2tog, yo sequence is followed by a purl stitch, the yo should be worked by taking the yarn from the back of the work to the front over the right-hand needle, rather than taking the yarn from the front of the work to the back around the right-hand needle as for a working a standard yo. On the following row, work into the back of this yob loop. For further background about yarn overs, *please see* the link to Ysolda Teague's blog post on the technique provided in the Bibliography (with thanks to Ysolda Teague).

Stitch Patterns

Use charted or written patterns, as preferred.

Note: The stitch patterns are worked in sections of 16 rows. Within these 16 rows, Patterns A and B, which consist of 16 rows, are worked once; Patterns C and D, which consist of 8 rows, are worked twice.

Pattern A, increasing from 1st to 9sts over 16 rows
Row 1 (RS): Yob, p1. (2sts, with 1st inc'd)
Row 2 (WS): Knit.
Row 3: Yob, p2. (3sts, with 1st inc'd)
Row 4: Knit.
Row 5: Yob, p3. (4sts, with 1st inc'd)
Row 6: Knit.
Row 7: Yob, p2, k2tog, yo. (5sts, with 1st inc'd)
Row 8: K1, p1, k3.
Row 9: Yob, p2, k2tog, yob, p1. (6sts, with 1st inc'd)
Row 10: K2, p1, k3.
Row 11: Yob, p2, k2tog, yob, p2. (7sts, with 1st inc'd)
Row 12: K3, p1, k3.
Row 13: Yob, p2, k2tog, yob, p3. (8sts, with 1st inc'd)
Row 14: K4, p1, k3.
Row 15: (Yob, p2, k2tog) × 2, yo. (9sts, with 1st inc'd)
Row 16: K1, (p1, k3) × 2.

Pattern B, increasing from 1st to 9sts over 16 rows
Row 1 (RS): P1, yo. (2sts, with 1st inc'd)
Row 2 (WS): Knit.

Row 3: P2, yo. (3sts, with 1st inc'd)
Row 4: Knit.
Row 5: P3, yo. (4sts, with 1st inc'd)
Row 6: Knit.
Row 7: Yo, ssk, p2, yo. (5sts, with 1st inc'd)
Row 8: K3, p1, k1.
Row 9: P1, yo, ssk, p2, yo. (6sts, with 1st inc'd)
Row 10: K3, p1, k2.
Row 11: P2, yo, ssk, p2, yo. (7sts, with 1st inc'd)
Row 12: K3, p1, k3.
Row 13: P3, yo, ssk, p2, yo. (8sts, with 1st inc'd)
Row 14: K3, p1, k4.
Row 15: (Yo, ssk, p2) × 2, yo. (9sts, with 1st inc'd)
Row 16: (K3, p1) × 2, k1.

Pattern C, worked over 8sts and 8 rows
Row 1 (RS): K1, k2tog, yob, p2, k2tog, yob, p1. (8sts)
Row 2 (WS): K2, p1, k3, p2.
Row 3: (K2tog, yob, p2) × 2.
Row 4: (K3, p1) × 2.
Row 5: K1, p2, k2tog, yob, p3.
Row 6: K4, p1, k2, p1.
Row 7: K1, p1, k2tog, yob, p2, k2tog, yo.
Row 8: K1, p1, k3, p1, k1, p1.

Close-up of the Open Doors Shawl triangle detail.

Pattern D, worked over 8sts and 8 rows
Row 1 (RS): P1, yo, ssk, p2, yo, ssk, k1. (8sts)
Row 2 (WS): P2, k3, p1, k2.
Row 3: (P2, yo, ssk) × 2.
Row 4: (P1, k3) × 2.
Row 5: P3, yo, ssk, p2, k1.
Row 6: P1, k2, p1, k4.
Row 7: Yo, ssk, p2, yo, ssk, p1, k1.
Row 8: P1, k1, p1, k3, p1, k1.

Pattern Instructions

Triangle set-up
Using 4mm needles, cast on 5sts.
Row 1 (RS): Sl1, k to end.
Row 2 (WS): Sl1 wyif, p to end.
Row 3: Sl1, k1, yo, k1, yo, k2. (7sts, with 2sts inc'd)
Row 4: Sl1 wyif, (p1, k1) twice, p2.
Row 5: Sl1, k1, p1, yo, k1, yob, p1, k2. (9sts, with 2sts inc'd)
Row 6: Sl1 wyif, p1, k1, p3, k1, p2.
Row 7: Sl1, k1, p1, k1, yo, k1, yo, k1, p1, k2. (11sts, with 2sts inc'd)
Row 8: Sl1 wyif, (p1, k1) four times, p2.
Row 9: Sl1, (k1, p1) twice, yo, k1, yob, p1, k1, p1, k2. (13sts, with 2sts inc'd)
Row 10: Sl1 wyif, (p1, k1) twice, p3, k1, p1, k1, p2.
Row 11: Sl1, (k1, p1) twice, (k1, yo) twice, (k1, p1) twice, k2. (15sts, with 2sts inc'd)
Row 12: Sl1 wyif, (p1, k1) six times, p2.
Row 13: Sl1, (k1, p1) twice, k1, yob, p1, k1, p1, yo, (k1, p1) twice, k2. (17sts, with 2sts inc'd)
Row 14: Sl1 wyif, (p1, k1) twice, p2, (k1, p1, k1, p2) twice.
Row 15: Sl1, (k1, p1) twice, k1, yo, (k1, p1) twice, k1, yo, (k1, p1) twice, k2. (19sts, with 2sts inc'd)
Row 16: Sl1 wyif, (p1, k1) eight times, p2.

Patterns A and B set-up
Row 1 (RS, placing 2 stitch markers for centre panel): Sl1, (k1, p1) twice, k1, work Pattern A row 1, pm, (k1, p1) twice, k1, pm, work Pattern B row 1, (k1, p1) twice, k2. (21sts, with 2sts inc'd)
Row 2 (WS): Sl1 wyif, (p1, k1) twice, p1, work Pattern B row 2, (p1, k1) twice, p1, work Pattern A row 2, (p1, k1) twice, p2.

Row 3: Sl1, (k1, p1) twice, k1, work Pattern A row 3, (k1, p1) twice, k1, work Pattern B row 3, (k1, p1) twice, k2. (23sts, with 2sts inc'd)

Continue as set by the previous 2 rows, working following row of both Pattern A and Pattern B for each subsequent row as required, until row 16 of both stitch patterns has been completed. (35sts when row 16 has been completed)

Triangle main pattern
Row 1 (RS, placing 2 additional stitch markers): Sl1, (k1, p1) twice, k1, work Pattern A row 1, pm, *work Pattern C row 1; rep from * to second mrk, (k1, p1) twice, k1, *work Pattern D row 1; rep from * to last 7sts, pm, work Pattern B row 1, (k1, p1) twice, k2. (37sts, with 2sts inc'd)
Row 2 (WS): Sl1 wyif, (p1, k1) twice, p1, work Pattern B row 2, *work Pattern D row 2; rep from * to second mrk, (p1, k1) twice, p1, *work Pattern C row 2; rep from * to fourth mrk, work Pattern A row 2, (p1, k1) twice, p2.
Row 3: Sl1, (k1, p1), twice, k1, work Pattern A row 3, *work Pattern C row 3; rep from * to second mrk, (k1, p1) twice, k1, *work Pattern D row 3; rep from * to fourth mrk, work Pattern B row 3, (k1, p1) twice, k2. (39sts, with 2sts inc'd)

Continue as set by the previous 2 rows, working following row of each of the four stitch patterns for each subsequent row of shawl body as required; work until all 16 rows of both Pattern A and Pattern B have been completed once and all 8 rows of both Pattern C and Pattern D have been completed twice. (51sts when sixteenth row of this section has been completed)

Leaving second and third markers in place for centre panel, remove first and fourth stitch markers while working the sixteenth row.

The previous 16 rows set the triangle main pattern.
Next, work the triangle main pattern another six times. (147sts)
Next, work rows 1–8 of the triangle main pattern once. (155sts)

Close-up of the Open Doors Shawl back-of-neck detail.

Centre back-of-neck shaping
Continuing as established by the triangle main pattern and keeping Patterns A, B, C and D correct, increase as follows at centre of shawl:
Row 9 (RS): Patt to second mrk, k1, p1, yo, k1, yob, p1, k1, patt to end. (159sts, with 4sts inc'd)
Row 10 (WS): Patt to second mrk, p1, k1, p3, k1, p1, patt to end.
Row 11: Patt to second mrk, k1, p1, k1, yo, k1, yo, k1, p1, k1, patt to end. (163sts, with 4sts inc'd)
Row 12: Patt to second mrk, (p1, k1) four times, p1, patt to end.
Row 13: Patt to second mrk, (k1, p1) twice, yo, k1, yob, (p1, k1) twice, patt to end. (167sts, with 4sts inc'd)
Row 14: Patt to second mrk, (p1, k1) twice, p3, (k1, p1) twice, patt to end.
Row 15: Patt to second mrk, (k1, p1) twice, k1, kfb, k1, (p1, k1) twice, patt to end. (170sts, with 3sts inc'd)
Row 16: Patt to second mrk, (p1, k1) twice, p4, (k1, p1) twice, patt to end.
Next, remove all four stitch markers.

Right back-of-neck shaping
Note: As neck shaping progresses, partial repeats of Pattern C are worked at the end of every RS row and

beginning of every WS row. For these partial repeats, if it is not possible to work all of a k2tog, yob or k2tog, yo decrease–increase sequence, knit or purl each stitch as necessary to maintain the established patterning of Pattern C (for example, knit a stitch that would have been included in a k2tog and purl a stitch that is in the position of what would have been a yob or yo).

Set-up

Row 1 (RS, placing new first mrk of row and dividing stitches for right and left sides of shawl): Sl1, (k1, p1) twice, k1, work Pattern A row 1, pm, patt 69sts by referring to Pattern C row 1, p2tog, k2tog, p1, k1, p1, k2, turn work, and place remaining 85sts (for shawl left side), in order, on to a spare needle or stitch holder. (84sts for shawl right side, with 1st inc'd and 2sts dec'd)

Row 2 (WS): Sl1 wyif, (p1, k1) three times, patt to mrk by referring to Pattern C row 2, work Pattern A row 2, (p1, k1) twice, p2.

Row 3: Sl1, (p1, k1) twice; work Pattern A row 3, patt to last 9sts by referring to Pattern C row 3, p2tog, k2tog, p1, k1, p1, k2. (83sts, with 1st inc'd and 2sts dec'd)

Continue as set by the previous 2 rows, working following row of both stitch patterns for each subsequent row of right back-of-neck shaping as required; work until all 16 rows of Pattern A have been completed once and all 8 rows of Pattern C have been completed twice. (77sts when sixteenth row of this section has been completed)

Remove stitch marker while working the sixteenth ow.

Main right back-of-neck pattern

Row 1: Sl1, (p1, k1) twice, work Pattern A row 1, pm, patt to last 9sts by referring to Pattern C row 1, p2tog, k2tog, p1, k1, p1, k2. (76sts, with 1st inc'd and 2sts dec'd)

Rows 2–16: Work as set by set-up rows 2–16, using Pattern A rows 2–16 and Pattern C rows 2–8 as required. (69sts)

Remove stitch marker while working row 16.

The previous 16 rows set the right back-of-neck shaping, with 1st being increased at the beginning and 2sts being decreased at the end of every RS row.

Next, work the right-back-of-neck shaping once. (61sts when row 16 has been completed)

Right bias rectangle

Row 1 (RS, placing first mrk of row): Sl1, (k1, p1) twice, k1, work Pattern A row 1, pm, patt to last 7sts by referring to Pattern C row 1, k2tog, p1, k1, p1, k2. (61sts, with 1st inc'd and 1st dec'd)

Row 2 (WS): Sl1 wyif, (p1, k1) twice, p1, patt to mrk by referring to Pattern C row 2, work Pattern A row 2, (p1, k1) twice, p2.

Row 3: Sl1, (k1, p1) twice, k1, work Pattern A row 3, patt to last 7sts by referring to Pattern C row 3, k2tog, p1, k1, p1, k2.

Continue as set by the previous 2 rows, working following row of both stitch patterns for each subsequent row of right bias rectangle as required, until all 16 rows of Pattern A have been completed once and all 8 rows of Pattern C have been completed twice. Remove stitch marker while working the sixteenth row.

The previous 16 rows set the right-bias-rectangle pattern, with 1st being increased at the beginning and 1st being decreased at the end of every RS row.

Next, work the right-bias-rectangle pattern another six times. Remove stitch marker while working the final row.

Right-rectangle shaping

Note: As shaping progress, partial repeats of Pattern C are worked at the beginning and end of every row. For these partial repeats, as earlier, if it is not possible to work all of a k2tog, yob or k2tog, yo decrease–increase sequence, knit or purl each stitch as necessary to maintain the established patterning of Pattern C.

Row 1 (RS): Sl1, (k1, p1) twice, ssk, patt to last 7sts by referring to Pattern C row 1, k2tog, p1, k1, p1, k2. (59sts, with 2sts dec'd)

Row 2 (WS): Sl1 wyif, (p1, k1) twice, p1, patt to last 6sts by referring Pattern C row 2, (p1, k1) twice, p2.

The previous 2 rows set the right-rectangle-shaping

Detail of the Open Doors Shawl rectangle points.

pattern, with 1st being decreased at the beginning and 1st being decreased at the end of every RS row.

Next, work the right-rectangle-shaping pattern another twenty-three times (46 rows), working following row of Pattern C for each subsequent row of right-rectangle shaping. (13sts when row 48 has been completed)

Right-rectangle point
Row 1 (RS): Sl1, (k1, p1) twice, sl1, k2tog, psso, p1, k1, p1, k2. (11sts, with 2sts dec'd)
Row 2 (WS): Sl1 wyif, p1, k1, p1, k3tog, p1, k1, p2. (9sts, with 2sts dec'd)
Row 3: Sl1, k1, p1, sl1, k2tog, psso, p1, k2. (7sts, with 2sts dec'd)
Row 4: Sl1 wyif, p1, k3tog, p2. (5sts, with 2sts dec'd)
Row 5: K1, sl1, k2tog, psso, k1. (3sts, with 2sts dec'd)
Row 6: Sl1, k2tog, psso. (1st, with 2sts dec'd)
Fasten off.

Left back-of-neck shaping
Note: As neck shaping progresses, partial repeats of Pattern D are worked at the beginning of every RS row and end of every WS row. For these partial repeats, if it is not possible to work all of a yo, ssk increase–decrease sequence, knit or purl each stitch as necessary to maintain the established patterning of Pattern D (for example, purl a stitch that is in the position of what would have been a yo and knit a stitch that would have been included in a ssk).

Return 85sts on spare needle or stitch holder to working needle, and, with RS facing, join yarn to first stitch at right-hand side of working needle.

Set-up
Row 1 (RS, placing new first mrk of row): Sl1, (k1, p1) twice, ssk, p2tog-tbl, patt to last 7sts by referring to Pattern D row 1, pm, work Pattern B row 1, (k1, p1) twice, k2. (84sts, with 1st inc'd and 2sts dec'd)
Row 2 (WS): Sl1 wyif, (p1, k1) twice, p1, work Pattern B row 2, patt to last 7sts by referring to Pattern D row 2, (k1, p1) three times, p1.
Row 3: Sl1, (k1, p1) twice, ssk, p2tog-tbl, patt to mrk by referring to Pattern D row 3, work Pattern B row 3 once, (k1, p1) twice, k2. (83sts, with 1st inc'd and 2sts dec'd)

Continue as set by previous 2 rows, working following row of both stitch patterns for each subsequent row of left back-of-neck shaping as required; work until all 16 rows of Pattern B have been completed once and all 8 rows of Pattern D have been completed twice. (77sts when sixteenth row of this section has been completed)

Remove stitch marker while working the sixteenth row.

Main left back-of-neck pattern
Row 1: Sl1, (k1, p1) twice, ssk, p2tog-tbl, patt to last 7sts by referring to Pattern D row 1, pm, work Pattern B row 1, (k1, p1) twice, k2. (76sts, with 1st inc'd and 2sts dec'd)
Rows 2–16: Work as set by set-up rows 2–3, using Pattern B rows 2–16 and Pattern D rows 2–8 as required. (69sts)

The Open Doors Shawl worn overlapped over one shoulder.

Remove stitch marker while working row 16.

The previous 16 rows set the left back-of-neck shaping, with 1st being increased at the end and 2sts being decreased at the beginning of every RS row.

Next, work the left-back-of-neck shaping once. (61sts when row 16 has been completed)

Left bias rectangle
Row 1 (RS, placing first mrk of row): Sl1, (k1, p1) twice, ssk, patt to last 7sts by referring to Pattern D row 1, pm, work Pattern B row 1, (k1, p1) twice, k2. (61sts, with 1st inc'd and 1st dec'd)
Row 2 (WS): Sl1 wyif, (p1, k1) twice, p1, work Pattern B row 2, patt to last 6sts by referring to Pattern D row 2, (p1, k1) twice, p2.
Row 3: Sl1, (k1, p1) twice, ssk, patt to mrk by referring to Pattern D row 3, work Pattern B row 3, (k1, p1) twice, k2.

Continue as set by the previous 2 rows, working following row of both stitch patterns for each subsequent row of left bias rectangle as required, until all 16 rows of Pattern B have been completed once and all 8 rows of Pattern D have been completed twice. Remove stitch marker while working the sixteenth row.

The previous 16 rows set the left-bias-rectangle pattern, with 1st being decreased at the beginning and 1st being increased at the end of every RS row.

Next, work the left-bias-rectangle pattern another six times. Remove stitch marker while working the final row.

Left-rectangle shaping
Note: As shaping progress, partial repeats of Pattern D are worked at the beginning and end of every row. For these partial repeats, as earlier, if it is not possible to work all of a yo, ssk increase–decrease sequence, knit or purl each stitch as necessary to maintain the established patterning of Pattern D.

Row 1 (RS): Sl1, (k1, p1) twice, ssk, patt to last 7sts by referring to Pattern D row 1, k2tog, (p1, k1) twice, k1. (59sts, with 2sts dec'd)
Row 2 (WS): Sl1 wyif, (p1, k1) twice, p1, patt to last 6sts by referring to Pattern D row 2, (p1, k1) twice, p2.

The previous 2 rows set the left-rectangle-shaping pattern, with 1st being decreased at the beginning and 1st being decreased at the end of every RS row.

Next, work the left-rectangle-shaping pattern another twenty-three times (46 rows), working following row of Pattern D for each subsequent row of left-rectangle shaping. (13sts when row 48 has been completed)

Left-rectangle point
Row 1 (RS): Sl1, (k1, p1) twice, k3tog, p1, k1, p1, k2. (11sts, with 2sts dec'd)
Row 2 (WS): Sl1 wyif, p1, k1, p1, k3tog, p1, k1, p2. (9sts, with 2sts dec'd)
Row 3: Sl1, k1, p1, k3tog, p1, k2. (7sts, with 2sts dec'd)
Row 4: Sl1 wyif, p1, k3tog, p2. (5sts, with 2sts dec'd)
Row 5: K1, k3tog, k1. (3sts, with 2sts dec'd)
Row 6: Sl1, k2tog, psso. (1st, with 2sts dec'd)
Fasten off.

Finishing
Sew in all loose ends. Block work gently to measurements given and according to instructions on yarn ball band.

CHAPTER 13

LAS SETAS SHAWL

Design Details

Inspiration

Located in the Plaza de la Encarnación in the centre of the Old Town of Seville, Las Setas is an enormous wooden structure designed by the Berlin-based architect Jürgen Mayer and opened in May 2011. The structure provides shade for the plaza below and is also home to the Mercado de la Encarnación and the Antiquarium Museum.

The structure of Las Setas influences three aspects of this shawl design: the overall shape of the shawl, the stitch pattern and the colour choice.

Shape

The segments of Las Setas provide the inspiration for the different segments of the shawl, which together comprise a crescent shape overall. This is similar to a modular design, although in this case the shawl is knitted lengthwise. The crescent is created by using short-row shaping within and between each shawl segment. The first segments are worked in groups of five, with each group including additional short rows and centre-eyelet-section rows. This allows the shawl to gradually grow in size. Once the full depth is reached, a single centre segment is worked before the segment

size is gradually decreased. The accompanying rough sketch demonstrates the initial idea and calculations for the layout and numbering of the segments. The stitch counts along the lower edge reflect the gradual increases and decreases.

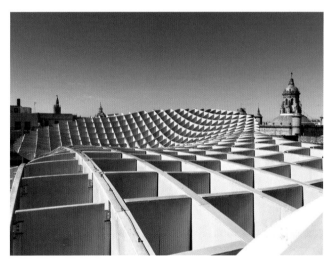

View across the top of Las Setas, Seville, Spain.

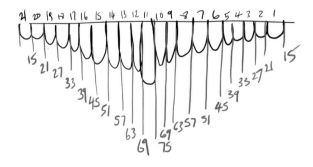

Rough sketch of the Las Setas Shawl construction, with stitch counts.

OPPOSITE: View from underneath Las Setas, Seville, Spain.

Design development

Las Setas is also known as 'The Mushrooms' and the 'Metropol Parasol', because its structure comprises six wide wooden parasols arranged around two large concrete columns. The individual shawl segments are inspired by these parasols. Short rows worked within each segment create shapes that are narrower at the inner edge of the shawl and wider at the outer edge. Stitches are increased and decreased at the outer edge of the segments to form the scalloped edges of the shawl.

When Las Setas is viewed from the plaza at ground level, hints of bright-blue sky are visible through the open sections of the structure. This is represented in the shawl design by narrow sections of short rows worked between each segment with a contrasting yarn shade.

Each individual shawl segment is knitted with an eyelet-mesh pattern surrounded by garter stitch. These stitch patterns are inspired by the open sections and the supporting structures of Las Setas, respectively, and are worked over different numbers of stitches and rows as the shawl segments increase, and decrease, in size.

Yarn and swatching

As the sun moves across Las Setas during the course of the day, the colour of the whole structure appears to gradually change. This aspect is represented in the yarn-colour choices for the test swatch and the final

The Rosa Pomar Mungo yarn used for the Las Setas swatch.

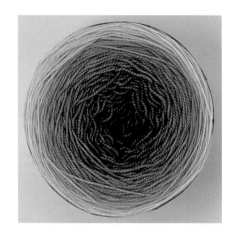

The Bilum yarn used for the Las Setas Shawl.

shawl. Two strongly contrasting shades represent the light in the middle of the day, when a deep-blue Spanish sky surrounds the golden structure. The subtle colours throughout a gradient yarn represent the gradual change from early morning light to an evening glow.

A test swatch is a very effective way to preview a design with the chosen project yarn before beginning the full shawl pattern. The same design can be worked with completely different yarn and yet still retain the essence of the original idea.

When considering a suitable yarn for working the Las Setas Shawl, the key considerations are structure and colour. The yarn selected for the test swatch is Rosa Pomar Mungo. This yarn has interesting texture, as it consists of a blend of recycled cotton and wool fibres, and it is available in shades that compliment the colour inspiration of the design; the chosen contrasting yarn shades of blue and yellow in turn represent the uninterrupted blue of the sky and the intense midday sunshine shown in the source images.

The yarn selected for the final shawl design is a Bilum hand-dyed merino yarn, Snek. This yarn provides both excellent stitch definition and structure, along with a long colour-change gradient. Using a slightly larger needle size than recommended on the ball band has the effect of creating a structured knitted fabric with excellent drape.

Both yarn choices suit the design requirements of colour and structure. Working the test swatch allows the knitter to choose the most suitable yarn for their own requirements.

Swatch Information

Inspiration: Las Setas, Seville, Spain

Shape: Crescent

Increase: Yo

Decreases: K2tog, ssk

Start: Cast-on edge of Segment 1 of swatch

Centre: Single segment

End: Cast-off edge of Segment 3 of swatch

Border (outer): Scalloped edge formed by increasing and decreasing

Border (inner): Garter stitch

Test yarn shown: Rosa Pomar Mungo (50-per-cent recycled wool, 50-per-cent recycled cotton, 220m/241yd per 100g ball)

End 1: Shade 005 (yellow); 1 × 100g ball, approximately 20g required for three-segment swatch

End 2: Shade 008 (blue); 1 × 100g ball, approximately 5g required for three-segment swatch

Needles: A pair 5mm (UK 6/US 8) knitting needles

Swatch Instructions (Three Segments)

Refer to main Las Setas Shawl Pattern Instructions throughout.

Use yarn of choice with appropriate needle size.

Segment 1

Work as for Pattern Instructions for Set-Up to end of Segment 1. (21sts)

Segment 2

Work as for Segment 1 rows 1–10, including the short rows.

Next, work as for Segment 17 rows 11–14.

Segment 3

Work as for Segment 21, including the cast-off.

Block swatch according to instructions on yarn ball band.

Las Setas swatch, knitted with 5mm needles and Rosa Pomar Mungo yarn.

Centre section of the Las Setas Shawl.

Size

39cm/15¼in (centre-segment depth) × 150cm/59in (curved top edge)

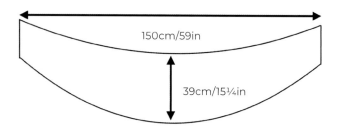

Blocking diagram for the Las Setas Shawl.

150cm/59in

39cm/15¼in

The Las Setas Shawl, fully extended.

Yarn

Bilum Snek (100-per-cent merino wool, 730m/798yd per 200g ball)

One-of-a-kind hand-dyed shades; 1 × 200g cake
Yarn amounts given are based on average requirements and are approximate.

Accessories

A pair 4mm (UK 8/US 6) knitting needles

Tensions

21sts × 48 rows to 10cm/4in × 10cm/4in over garter-stitch pattern (*see* Stitch Patterns), using 4mm needles
21sts × 31 rows to 10cm/4in × 10cm/4in over stocking-stitch pattern, using 4mm needles
Use larger or smaller needles as necessary to obtain correct tension.

Pattern Notes

Reverse-gradient effect: The shawl has a reverse-gradient effect that is created by using each end of the Bilum cake of yarn. End 1 is of the lightest shade and taken from the outside of the cake. End 2 is of the darkest shade and taken from the centre of the cake. If using separate balls of yarn, choose the lightest shade for End 1 and the darkest shade for End 2. When working with both ends of the same yarn source, in this case a yarn cake, turn the work carefully at the end of each row, to avoid making unnecessary twists in the yarn. Every so often, it is likely to be necessary to stop and untangle any unexpected twisting around one another of the two yarn ends.

Managing yarn ends: As End 1 and End 2 are used alternately throughout the shawl, to avoid having to repeatedly cut the yarn, loosely carry the end not in use up the side of the work, twisting it together with the working end at the start of each row; be careful not to pull this stranded yarn too tightly, to avoid reducing the elasticity of the shawl's inner edge. Alternatively, if preferred, End 1 can be cut when switching to using End 2, and vice versa, and the resulting yarn ends can later be woven into the adjacent stitches of the same colour on the wrong side of the work. However, it is strongly recommended that you do not repeatedly cut the yarn ends – developing an efficient and tidy technique to twist and therefore catch in the yarn not in use is a very handy skill.

Short-row (SR) shaping: Short-row shaping is used within each segment and between each segment. A stitch is wrapped to avoid a gap remaining in the knitting where each short row is worked. This wrapping action is known as wrap and turn, 'w&t'. For this pattern, to wrap a stitch, knit to the stitch to be wrapped; slip the next stitch purlwise; take the yarn to the back of the work; slip the slipped stitch back to the left-hand needle purlwise without working it; take the yarn to the front of the work; and turn the work. When the wrapped stitch is reached on the subsequent row,

The reverse side of the Las Setas Shawl.

The Las Setas Shawl Segments 1–5.

work the wrap loop and the wrapped stitch together to close the gap between the wrapped stitch and the adjacent stitch.

The knitted segments worked with short-row shaping of the Las Setas Shawl.

Stitch Patterns

Garter-Stitch Pattern
Knit every row.

Eyelet Pattern, with repeat worked over multiples of 2sts and 2 rows
Row 1 (RS): Sl1, ssk, yo, k1, *yo, k2tog; rep from * to last st, k1.
Row 2 (WS): Sl1, k to end.

Pattern Instructions

Set-up
Using 4mm needles and End 1, cast on 15sts.
Row 1 (RS): Sl1, k to end.
Row 2 (WS): Work as row 1.

Segment 1
Side eyelet section
Rows 1–2: Work as Eyelet Pattern rows 1–2.

Increase and SR section
Row 3 (RS): Sl1, ssk, yo, k to last 2sts, yo, k2. (16sts, with 1st inc'd)

Row 4: Work SRs within this row as follows:
SR1 (WS): Sl1, k to last 5sts, w&t;
SR2, 4 and 6 (RS): K to last 2sts, yo, k2. (19sts after SR6 has been completed, with 3sts inc'd in total);
SR3: Sl1, k to last 7sts, w&t;
SR5: Sl1, k to last 9sts, w&t;
SR7: Sl1, k to end of row.

Centre eyelet section
Rows 5–8: Work as Eyelet Pattern rows 1–2.

Decrease and SR section
Row 9 (RS): Sl1, ssk, yo, k to last 5sts, k2tog, yo, k2tog, k1. (18sts, with 1st dec'd)
Row 10: Work SRs within this row as follows:
SR1 (WS): Sl1, k to last 9sts, w&t;
SR2, 4 and 6 (RS): K to last 5sts, k2tog, yo, k2tog, k1. (15sts after SR6 has been completed, with 3sts dec'd in total);
SR3: Sl1, k to last 7sts, w&t;
SR5: Sl1, k to last 5sts, w&t;
SR7: Sl1, k to end of row.

Side eyelet section
Rows 11–12: Work as Eyelet Pattern rows 1–2.

Contrast-colour SR section
Note that both End 1 and End 2 are used within this section, as indicated. Once both yarn ends are in use, you are strongly encouraged to loosely strand the yarn end not in use and to twist it together with the working end (*see Pattern Notes: Managing yarn ends*); conversely, it is not recommended to repeatedly cut the yarn ends.
Row 13: Work SRs within this row as follows:
SR1 (RS): Using End 2, sl1, ssk, yo, k to last 7sts, w&t;
SR2, 4 and 6 (WS): Using End 2, p to last 3sts, k3;
SR3: Using End 2, sl1, ssk, yo, k to last 5sts, w&t;
SR5: Using End 2, sl1, ssk, yo, k to last 7sts, w&t;
SR7: Using End 1, sl1, ssk, yo, k to last 3sts, yo, k2tog, k1.

Cast-on of stitches for working of following segment
Row 14 (WS): Cast on 6sts at beginning of row, sl1, k to end. (21sts, with 6sts inc'd)

Segments 2–5

The previous 14 rows (including the three intervening sets of SRs1–7) set the pattern for Segments 2–5. Note that the stated stitch counts for rows 1–14 are relevant only when these rows are being worked for the first time. Work these 14 rows another four times to complete these segments and to increase for working Segment 6. (45sts after Segment 5 has been completed)

Segment 6

Side eyelet section

Rows 1–2: Work as Eyelet Pattern rows 1–2.

Increase and SR section

Row 3 (RS): Sl1, ssk, yo, k to last 2sts, yo, k2. (46sts, with 1st inc'd)

Row 4: Work SRs within this row as follows:

SR1 (WS): Sl1, k to last 5sts, w&t;

SR2, 4, 6, 8 and 10 (RS): K to last 2sts, yo, k2. (51sts after SR10 has been completed, with 5sts inc'd in total);

SR3: Sl1, k to last 7sts, w&t;

SR5: Sl1, k to last 9sts, w&t;

SR7: Sl1, k to last 11sts, w&t;

SR9: Sl1, k to last 13sts, w&t;

SR11: Sl1, k to end of row.

Centre eyelet section

Rows 5–10: Work as Eyelet Pattern rows 1–2.

Decrease and SR section

Row 11 (RS): Sl1, ssk, yo, k to last 5sts, k2tog, yo, k2tog, k1. (50sts, with 1st dec'd)

Row 12: Work SRs within this row as follows:

SR1 (WS): Sl1, k to last 13sts, w&t;

SR2, 4, 6, 8 and 10 (RS): K to last 5sts, k2tog, yo, k2tog, k1. (45sts after SR10 has been completed, with 5sts dec'd in total);

SR3: Sl1, k to last 11sts, w&t;

SR5: Sl1, k to last 9sts, w&t;

SR7: Sl1, k to last 7sts, w&t;

SR9: Sl1, k to last 5sts, w&t;

SR11: Sl1, k to end of row.

The Las Setas Shawl Segments 10–21.

Side eyelet section

Rows 13–14: Work as Eyelet Pattern rows 1–2.

Contrast-colour SR section

Note that both End 1 and End 2 are used within this section, as indicated.

Row 15: Work SRs within this row as follows:

SR1 (RS): Using End 2, sl1, ssk, yo, k to last 7sts, w&t;

SR2, 4 and 6 (WS): Using End 2, p to last 3sts, k3;

SR3: Using End 2, sl1, ssk, yo, k to last 5sts, w&t;

SR5: Using End 2, sl1, ssk, yo, k to last 7sts, w&t;

SR7: Using End 1, sl1, ssk, yo, k to last 3sts, yo, k2tog, k1.

Cast-on of stitches for working of following segment

Row 16 (WS): Cast on 6sts at beginning of row, sl1, k to end. (51sts, with 6sts inc'd)

Segments 7–10

The previous 16 rows (including the intervening sets of SRs1–11, SRs1–11 and SRs1–7) set the pattern for Segments 7–10. Note that the stated stitch counts for rows 1–16 are relevant only when these rows are being worked for the first time.

Work these 16 rows another four times to complete these segments and to increase for working Segment 11. (75sts after Segment 10 has been completed)

Segment 11 – centre segment
Rows 1–4: Work as Segment 6 rows 1–4.
Rows 5–12: Work as Eyelet Pattern rows 1–2.
Rows 13–14: Work as Segment 6 rows 11–12.

Side eyelet section
Row 15 (RS): Work as Eyelet Pattern row 1.
Row 16 (WS): Cast off 6sts at beginning of row, k to end. (69sts, with 6sts dec'd)

Contrast-colour SR section
Row 17 (RS): Work as Segment 6 row 15.
Row 18 (WS): Sl1, k to end.

Segment 12
Rows 1–4: Work as Segment 6 rows 1–4.
Rows 5–10: Work as Eyelet Pattern rows 1–2.
Rows 11–12: Work as Segment 6 rows 11–12.

Side eyelet section
Row 13 (RS): Work as Eyelet Pattern row 1.
Row 14 (WS): Cast off 6sts at beginning of row, k to end. (63sts, with 6sts dec'd)

Contrast-colour SR section
Row 15 (RS): Work as Segment 6 row 15.
Row 16 (WS): Sl1, k to end.

Segments 13–16
The previous 16 rows set the pattern for Segments 13–16. Note that the stated stitch count for row 14 is relevant only when this row is being worked for the first time.

Work these 16 rows another four times to complete these segments and to decrease for working Segment 17. (39sts after Segment 16 has been completed)

Segment 17
Rows 1–4: Work as Segment 1 rows 1–4.
Rows 5–8: Work as Eyelet Pattern rows 1–2.
Rows 9–10: Work as Segment 1 rows 9–10.

Side eyelet section
Row 11 (RS): Work as Eyelet Pattern row 1.
Row 12 (WS): Cast off 6sts at beginning of row, k to end. (33sts, with 6sts dec'd)

Contrast-colour SR section
Row 13 (RS): Work as Segment 1 row 13.
Row 14 (WS): Sl1, k to end.

Segments 18–20
The previous 14 rows set the pattern for Segments 18–20. Note that the stated stitch count for row 12 is relevant only when this row is being worked for the first time.

Work these 14 rows another three times to complete these segments and to decrease for working Segment 21. (15sts after Segment 20 has been completed)

Segment 21
Use End 1 only throughout.
Rows 1–4: Work as Segment 1 rows 1–4.
Rows 5–8: Work as Eyelet Pattern rows 1–2.
Rows 9–10: Work as Segment 1 rows 9–10.

Side eyelet section
Rows 11–12: Work as Eyelet Pattern rows 1–2.
Row 13 (RS): Sl1, ssk, yo, k to last 3sts, yo, k2tog, k1. Cast off knitwise with WS facing.

Finishing
Sew in all loose ends by weaving these ends into stitches of the same colour only on the wrong side of the work, to help to avoid the contrast-colour ends showing through to the right side. Block work to measurements given and according to instructions on yarn ball band.

BIBLIOGRAPHY

BOOKS

Black, S., *Knitting: Fashion, Industry, Craft* (V&A Publishing, 2012)

Braaten, A. and Strawn, S., 'Further Discoveries of Virginia Woods Bellamy's Geometric Number Knitting', *Piecework* (February 2020)

Bush, N., *Knitted Lace of Estonia* (Interweave Press, 2008)

Compton, R., *The Complete Book of Traditional Knitting* (Batsford Limited, 1983)

Corbould, E.M., *The Lady's Knitting Book* (Hatchards, 1874)

Corbould, E.M., *The Lady's Knitting Book* (Hatchards, 1878)

Corbould, E.M., *Mother's Knitter: containing some patterns for things for little children* (Hatchards, 1882)

Davies, K. and Arnall-Culliford, J. (eds), *The Book of Haps* (Kate Davies Designs, 2016)

Ellen, A., *Knitting: Stitch-Led Design* (The Crowood Press, 2015)

Gaugain, Mrs J., *The Lady's Assistant for Executing Useful and Fancy Designs in Knitting, Netting and Crochet Work*, third volume, fourth edition (I. J. Gaugain and Ackermann & Co., 1841)

Gaugain, Mrs J., *Lady's Assistant in Knitting, Netting and Crochet Work*, second volume (Ackermann & Co., 1842)

Gaugain, Mrs J., *The Lady's Workbook* (Edinburgh, 1842)

Historic Resources Group, City of Palm Springs, *Citywide Historic Context & Survey Findings* (2015)

Lambert, Miss F., *My Knitting Book* (J. Murray, 1844)

Lambert, Miss F., *My Knitting Book* (J. Murray, 1847)

Leapman, M., *Knitting Modular: Shawls, Wraps, and Stoles* (Storey Publishing, 2018)

Lorant, T., *Knitted Shawls and Wraps* (Thorn Press, 1984)

Mida, Dr I.E., *Reading Fashion in Art* (Bloomsbury, 2020)

Miller, S., *Heirloom Knitting* (Shetland Times Ltd, 2002)

Nargi, L., *Knitting Around the World* (Voyageur Press, 2011)

Ruutel, H. and Reimann, S., *Knitted Shawls of Helga Ruutel* (Saara Publishing House, 2013)

Sowerby, J., *Victorian Lace Today* (XRX Books, 2007)

Thomas, M., *Mary Thomas's Knitting Book* (Hodder and Stoughton, 1987)

Thomas, M., *Mary Thomas's Book of Knitting Patterns* (Dover Publications, 2015)

Woods Bellamy, V., *Number Knitting: The New All-Ways-Stretch Method* (Crown Publishers, 1952)

Zimmermann, E., *Elizabeth Zimmermann's Knitter's Almanac* (Dover Publications, 1981)

Zimmermann, E., *Knitting Workshop* (Schoolhouse Press, 1984)

Zimmermann, E. and Swansen, M. (eds), *Knitting Around* (Schoolhouse Press, 1989)

WEBSITES

Fashion and Textile Museum (FTM), London, https://www.ftmlondon.org

Knitting and Crochet Guild (KCG), https://kcguild.org.uk

Knitting Reference Library, University of Southampton, https://library.soton.ac.uk/wsa/KRL

Rijksmuseum Online Collection, https://www.rijksmuseum.nl/en

Stitchmastery, https://www.stitchmastery.com

The Victoria and Albert Museum (V&A) Collections, https://collections.vam.ac.uk

Victorian Knitting Manuals, University of Southampton, https://archive.org/details/victorianknittingmanuals

Ysolda Teague, 'How to knit more symmetrical yarnovers', https://ysolda.com/blogs/journal/how-to-knit-more-symmetrical-yarn-overs

YARN STOCKISTS

baa ram ewe, https://baaramewe.co.uk

Bilum, https://www.bilumyarns.com

Brooklyn Tweed, https://brooklyntweed.com

Carol Feller (Stolen Stitches), https://stolenstitches.com

Garthenor Organic, https://garthenor.com

Ida's House (from which the Bilum yarn was purchased), https://idashouse.co.uk

Irish Artisan Yarn, https://www.irish-artisan-yarn.com

John Arbon Textiles, https://www.jarbon.com

Tangled Yarn (from which the Carol Feller yarn was purchased), https://www.tangled-yarn.co.uk

Wollhaus (from which the Brooklyn Tweed yarn was purchased), https://www.wollhaus.com